PEOPLE AT ODDS

THE BALKANS: PEOPLE IN CONFLICT

PEOPLE AT ODDS

PEOPLE AT ODDS

THE BALKANS: PEOPLE IN CONFLICT

Hal Marcovitz

Chelsea House Publishers
Philadelphia

CHELSEA HOUSE PUBLISHERS

EDITOR IN CHIEF Sally Cheney
DIRECTOR OF PRODUCTION Kim Shinners
CREATIVE MANAGER Takeshi Takahashi
MANUFACTURING MANAGER Diann Grasse

Staff for THE **BALKANS: PEOPLE** IN **CONFLICT**

ASSISTANT EDITOR Susan Naab
PICTURE RESEARCHER Sarah Bloom
PRODUCTION ASSISTANT Jaimie Winkler
COVER AND SERIES DESIGNER Keith Trego
LAYOUT 21st Century Publishing and Communications, Inc.

http://www.chelseahouse.com

First Printing

1 3 5 7 9 8 6 4 2

Library of Congress Cataloging-in-Publication Data

Marcovitz, Hal.
   The Balkans : people in conflict / by Hal Marcovitz.
     p. cm. — (People at odds)
Includes bibliographical references and index.
   ISBN 0-7910-6710-6
1. Balkan Peninsula—History—Juvenile literature. I. Title. II. Series.
DR37 .M37 2002
949.6—dc21

                                                        2002000987

CONTENTS

F.Y.R.O.M. - The Former Yugoslav Republic of Macedonia

Barents
Sea

Jan Mayen
(NORWAY)

Greenland
Sea

ICELAND

Hammerfest

Tromsø

Murmansk

White Sea

Arkhar

Norwegian Sea

Arctic   Circle

Kiruna

Tórshavn   Faroe Islands
(DENMARK)

NORWAY

Luleå

Oulu

SWEDEN

Trondheim

FINLAND

Lake
Onega

SHETLAND
ISLANDS

Umeå

Tampere

Lake
Ladoga

Bergen

Oslo

Gävle

Turku Helsinki

St. Petersburg

RUSSIA

Mos

Rockall
(U.K.)

ORKNEY
ISLANDS

Stavanger

Stockholm

ÅLAND
ISLANDS

Tallinn
ESTONIA

HEBRIDES

Göteborg

Gotland

Rīga

LATVIA

Vitsyebsk

Smolensk

North

Aberdeen

North
Sea

Baltic Sea

Öland

LITHUANIA
Vilnius

Mahilyow

Minsk

Atlantic

Glasgow
Edinburgh

DENMARK
Copenhagen

Malmö

Kaliningrad

BELARUS

Ocean

Belfast

UNITED

Bornholm

RUSSIA

Hrodna

Homyel

Celtic
Sea

Dublin

Isle
of
Man
(U.K.)

Leeds
Manchester
Liverpool

Hamburg

Gdańsk

Warsaw

Brest

Kiev

IRELAND

KINGDOM

Cardiff

Birmingham

Amsterdam

NETH.

Bremen

Berlin

Poznań

POLAND

Rivne

UKRAINE

London

Rotterdam

Essen
Cologne

Leipzig

Łódź
Wrocław

L'viv

Guernsey (U.K.)
Jersey (U.K.)

Brussels
Lille

BEL.
Bonn

GERMANY

Prague

Kraków

Chernivtsi

Myk

Paris

LUX.
Luxembourg

Frankfurt
am Main

CZECH REPUBLIC

Brno

SLOVAKIA

CARPATHIAN MTS

Chişinău

Nantes

Stuttgart

Munich

Vienna

Bratislava

Iaşi
MOLDOVA

Strasbourg

LIECH.

AUSTRIA

Budapest

Cluj-
Napoca

Zürich
Bern
Geneva

Vaduz

HUNGARY

ROMANIA

Bay of
Biscay

FRANCE

MASSIF
CENTRAL

SWITZ.

Ljubljana

SLOVENIA

Zagreb

Bucharest

Con

Bordeaux

Lyon

Turin

Milan

Venice

CROATIA

Danube

Varna

Bilbao

Toulouse

Genoa

SAN
MARINO

Florence

BOSNIA AND
HERZEGOVINA

Belgrade

BULGARIA

Porto

PYRENEES

MONACO

Marseille

Ligurian
Sea

Sarajevo

YUGOSLAVIA

Sofia

İstanbul

Andorra
la Vella

Zaragoza

ANDORRA

ITALY
Rome

Adriatic
Sea

Tirana

Skopje
F.Y.R.O.M.

Thessaloniki

Bu

Madrid

Barcelona

VATICAN
CITY

ALB.

TUR

SPAIN

Valencia

Balearic
Sea

Sardinia

Naples

Tyrrhenian
Sea

GREECE

Aegean
Sea

İz

Sevilla

BALEARIC
ISLANDS

Cagliari

Athens

Rh

Gibraltar Málaga
(U.K.)

Mediterranean Sea

Palermo

Ionian
Sea

Ceuta
(SPAIN)

Alborán
Sea

Algiers

Sicily

Scale 1: 19,500,000
Lambert Conformal Conic Projection,
standard parallels 40 °N and 56 °N

Melilla
(SPAIN)

Oran

Tunis

Rabat

ALGERIA

TUNISIA

Valletta
MALTA

0   300 Kilometers

0   300 Miles

20

MOROCCO

Death of the Tiger

To his friends, Zeljko Raznatovic was a rich businessman with a celebrity wife and a love for soccer. He dined in fine restaurants, lived in a luxurious home in the Yugoslavian capital of Belgrade, and dabbled in national politics by serving in his country's Parliament.

But to the hapless victims of Yugoslavia's many wars against its Balkan neighbors, Raznatovic was a vicious killer known as "Arkan"—leader of the fierce paramilitary force named the Tigers. Dressed in military fatigues, Arkan enjoyed swaggering at the head of his troops, often holding aloft a baby tiger so that photographers would capture the image he hoped to convey —that of a merciless band of marauders specializing in the

The Balkan states are located along the eastern coast of the Adriatic Sea in Europe. They are bordered by Hungary, Austria, and Italy in the north, Albania and Greece in the south, and Bulgaria and Romania in the east.

Swaggering and ruthless, Serbian leader Zelijko Raznatovic lived a life of urban sophistication while simultaneously leading a band of paramilitary soldiers— dubbed The Tigers—on a vicious ethnic cleansing campaign. Known as "Arkan," he would often be photographed with a baby tiger to show the world the fierceness of his military force.

unique brand of warfare known as "ethnic cleansing."

In 1997, an international court sitting in The Hague, Netherlands, indicted Arkan on charges of committing a series of brutal war crimes against ethnic Muslims in Bosnia-Herzegovina and Croatia. Arkan, a onetime bank robber who was wanted by international police agencies, had organized his private army of thugs in 1991. Soon, they were put to work by Slobodan Milosevic, the Yugoslavian leader who dreamed of establishing a south Slavic empire ruled by Serbs. During the fighting that was to come in the republics of Croatia and Bosnia-Herzegovina, Arkan led the Tigers on vicious missions of hate, murdering innocent civilians, burning their homes, and looting their shops.

"Arkan was something special, a freelance murderer who roamed across Bosnia and [Croatia] with his black-shirted men, terrorizing Muslims and Croats," said Richard Holbrooke, an American diplomat who helped broker a peace treaty in the Balkans. "To the rest of the world Arkan was a racist fanatic run amok, but many Serbs regarded him as a hero. His private army, the Tigers, had committed some of the war's worst atrocities."

There were dozens of other paramilitary groups roaming the Balkans as well, and they often adopted the names of fearsome warriors as a way to strike terror in their enemies. Among those groups were the Yellow Wasps, Jokers, Falcons, and White Eagles.

There was no question, though, that the Tigers were the most vicious and relentless of the paramilitary fighters. Arkan recruited members from among the thugs and hooligans who were fans of the soccer team he owned, the Belgrade Obilic.

By 1992, the former Yugoslavia had disintegrated. All that remained of the nation forged of diverse ethnic groups at the end of World War II were the republics of Serbia and Montenegro and the lesser provinces of Kosovo and Vojvodina. The republics of Bosnia-Herzegovina, Macedonia, and Slovenia had voted to secede. In what was left of Yugoslavia, the Serbs made up the ethnic majority and dominated the government. Under Milosevic, the Serbs aimed to redraw the lines of the Balkans, creating a south Slavic empire under their rule.

In the spring of 1992 Arkan and the Tigers arrived at the cities of Bijeljina and Zvornik in Bosnia-Herzegovina. The two cities were regarded as key to Milosevic's plan of bringing together all southern Slavic people into a unified empire. During the breakup of the former Yugoslavia that started the year before, Serbs seethed as the territories surrounding the two cities remained within the borders of Bosnia-Herzegovina. They insisted that the regions, which included a large Bosnian Serb population, be made part of the Serbian republic.

And so Arkan led the Tigers to Bijeljina and Zvornik to take the cities and oust the ethnic population of Muslims, whom many Serbs had regarded as their sworn enemies since medieval times.

On April 1, the Tigers arrived at Bijeljina. They took up sniper positions around the city, patrolled the streets, and fired off machine-gun bursts at random. Soon, the harassment of the Muslims turned bloody. The Tigers went door-to-door in Bijeljina, hunting down Muslim leaders of the town government and shooting them on the spot.

"It was unbelievable almost," said Bosnia president Alija Izetbegovic, when he learned of the atrocities. "The civilians being killed, pictures showed dead bodies of the women in the streets. I thought it was a photo-montage, I couldn't believe my eyes, I couldn't believe it was possible."

Within days, the entire non-Serbian population of Bijeljina had either been murdered by the Tigers or had fled the city. The ethnic cleansing of Bijeljina was now complete.

Arkan and the Tigers were not finished. Next, they moved on to Zvornik, arriving at the outskirts of the city on April 8. As with Bijeljina, Zvornik had a large Muslim population. Already, word had reached the Muslims of Zvornik about the atrocities committed the week before in Bijeljina. Thousands of Muslims started to flee the city, heading for refugee camps in the Bosnian countryside.

Arkan opened fire on Zvornik two days later. Many Muslims were still trapped inside the city and found themselves the target of Arkan's terror. The Tigers stormed the city, pulling Muslims from their homes and executing them in the streets.

"I could see trucks full of dead bodies," said Jose María Mendiluce, a United Nations official who witnessed the carnage. "I could see militiamen taking more corpses of children, women and old people from their houses and putting them on trucks. I saw at least four or five trucks full of corpses. When I arrived the cleansing had been done. There were no people, no one on the streets. It was all finished. They were looting, cleaning up the city after the massacre. I was convinced they were going to kill me."

The United Nations worker was permitted to leave Zvornik. The story of what Mendiluce and others had seen in the streets of Bijeljina and Zvornik soon reached the international press. Leaders of democratic governments in the west expressed outrage and called for the butchers to be brought to justice. But in the halls of government in the Yugoslavian capital of Belgrade, the crimes committed by Arkan and the Tigers would fall on deaf ears.

When Western diplomats confronted President Slobodan Milosevic, the head of the government at first denied knowing Arkan. Holbrooke said that when he demanded answers about the activities of the Tigers, Milosevic dismissed Arkan's crimes as a "peanut issue."

"He [Milosevic] claimed he had no influence over him," Holbrooke said. "Arkan at large remained a dangerous force and a powerful signal that one could still get away with murder—literally—in Bosnia."

Despite Milosevic's denials, there was no question that Arkan and the Tigers were very much under the control of the Yugoslavian leader. In return, Arkan and his family enjoyed the favor of Milosevic's government. For example, Arkan was allowed to live in the plush residence of the ambassador of Thailand after the diplomat was recalled by his country.

"Arkan operated within the Territorial Defense system," said Dobrila Gajic-Glisic, the executive secretary to General Tomislav Simovic, head of the Yugoslavian military. "He had his own group which acted under his command, but all actions were cleared and coordinated with the Yugoslav army [high command]."

When army officers reported to Simovic that Arkan and the Tigers were committing atrocities, the general shrugged his shoulders. "I support anyone who is actively fighting," he said. "I'm not in a position to control who does what on the ground. I leave that to each man's conscience."

For the next eight years, Arkan lived openly and defiantly in Belgrade, getting rich by stealing oil from Muslim regions and selling it on the black market. As a businessman, Arkan's many holdings included the soccer team as well as ice cream parlors and clothing factories. His wife was the beautiful folksinger and recording star known as "Ceca."

As diplomatic efforts to bring Bosnia, Serbia, and Croatia to the peace table began to wane, U.S. Assistant Secretary of State Richard Holbrooke intervened diplomatically. Shown here with Bosnian Prime Minister Haris Silajdic and Bosnian President Alijia Izetbegovic, Holbrooke was especially frustrated with the Yugoslavian response to Arkan's ethnic cleansing.

Arkan and his wife often appeared on television together.

In politics, he helped establish the Serbian Unity Party and served in the Yugoslavian Parliament. Indeed, during his campaign for Parliament in 1993, he ran on the slogan: "Only Unity Can Save the Serbs."

As for the Tigers, they were always ready when he called. Throughout the regions of the Balkans controlled by the Serbs, the Tigers were regarded as valiant heroes.

A popular song played on radio stations included these lyrics:

> They protect Serb glory,
> They guard Serb lands,
> Arkan's Tigers,
> Brave warriors without a flaw.

Nevertheless, by 1997 international pressure to bring Arkan to justice was finally bearing fruit. At The Hague, the International Criminal Tribunal for the former Yugoslavia issued its indictment of Arkan on war crimes. Publicly, the head of the Tigers laughed off the indictment, defiantly stating that no court would bring him to justice.

"I didn't see any Serb doing any crime," Arkan told a reporter shortly after his indictment.

Privately, though, Arkan was believed to be very concerned about the net that was closing in on him. The North Atlantic Treaty Organization (NATO), the military alliance of western nations, started bombing Belgrade in March 1999 to halt the Yugoslavian army attacks on Kosovo, an autonomous region in Serbia composed of a large Muslim population. The Tigers were believed to be very much involved in ethnic cleansing in Kosovo. Unable to defend their country against the NATO onslaught, many Yugoslavian leaders feared the alliance would next send in ground troops—and that could lead to the arrests and trials of the men responsible for the atrocities of the past decade.

Arkan approached The Hague tribunal on his own. He wanted to know if he could receive amnesty for his crimes in exchange for testimony against Yugoslavian leaders. It was believed that his testimony would implicate some of Yugoslavia's most important leaders in war crimes— perhaps even Milosevic himself.

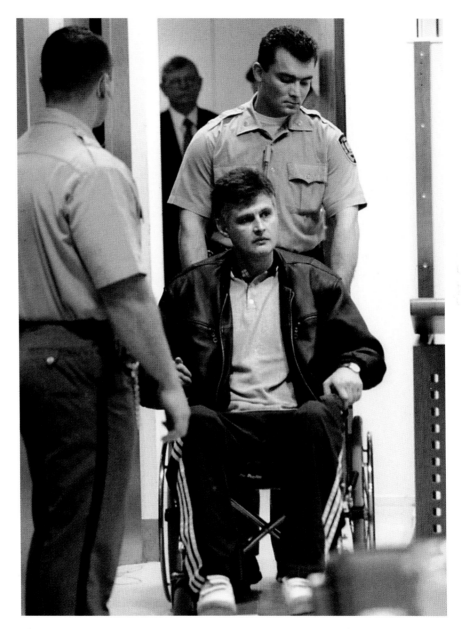

Confined to a wheelchair, Bosnian Serb war crimes suspect Milan Simic is wheeled into the courtroom at The Hague war crimes tribunal. He and fellow suspect Miroslav Tadic were the first to voluntary surrender to the tribunal, where they pleaded innocent to charges that they participated in a terror campaign in northern Bosnia.

But Arkan would never get the chance to tell what he knew.

On January 15, 2000, Arkan and two other men—Milenko Mandic and Dragan Garic—sat down for dinner in a restaurant just off the lobby of the Hotel Intercontinental in Belgrade. They finished dinner just after 5 P.M. Arkan, Mandic, and Garic stood at their table and prepared to leave the restaurant. Garic was at Arkan's side quite often; he served as bodyguard for the head of the Tigers. Mandic was a business associate.

A man approached the table. He was young—just 23 years old—and known to Arkan. The two men shook hands and embraced, then exchanged a few words. Their conversation over, Arkan left the table accompanied by Mandic and Garic. They had just stepped into the lobby of the Hotel Intercontinental when the young man walked up behind Arkan and shot him three times in the back of the head. The leader of the Tigers collapsed to the lobby floor. He would be pronounced dead minutes later in a hospital emergency room.

Mandic and Garic also lost their lives that day. Two other men had been waiting in the hotel lobby and they opened fire as well, killing the bodyguard and businessman. The three assassins then hurried past dozens of shocked people in the Intercontinental lobby and disappeared into the busy Belgrade streets.

A week later, Belgrade police announced the arrest of Arkan's assassin: Dobrosav Gavric, a former policeman, was identified as the man who walked up behind Arkan and pulled the trigger. Within a few months, nine other defendants were charged with participating in the conspiracy. All the defendants were convicted. Gavric received a sentence of 20 years in prison; the others were handed lesser penalties. All defendants refused to talk about who organized the conspiracy and whether the plot to kill Arkan was hatched at the top levels of the Yugoslavian government.

Judge Dragoljub Djordjevic, who presided over the trial, said he suspected the conspirators had been paid to maintain their silence.

"It is obvious some deal was involved, something was promised to the perpetrators, but we could not determine what or who may have ordered it," the judge said.

Later, it seemed that nobody who knew Arkan was much surprised at the news of his murder.

"The main question was not whether Arkan would be killed, but when," said Slavoljub Kacarevic, editor of the newspaper *Glas Javnosti.*

The Field
of Blackbirds

For Americans, the heroism shown by the Union and Confederate soldiers at the Battle of Gettysburg serves as a defining moment in their nation's history. The willingness of ordinary men to die in defense of their beliefs is regarded with solemn admiration by many American citizens.

Many citizens of Yugoslavia have similar feelings about the heroes of a military battle fought by the Serbs against the Ottoman Turks on June 28, 1389.

The Ottomans had ventured into eastern Europe some 40 years before, easily overrunning the armies of the Balkan states. The Ottomans had always stopped short of total conquest, though, preferring instead to maintain treaties with the Balkan kings. Such treaties were easily accomplished. The kings of Serbia, Bosnia, Macedonia, and the other states were suspicious and jealous of one another; they harbored ambitions of conquest themselves and saw treaties with the powerful Turks as opportunities to gain an advantage over their rivals.

18

The Balkan states—Croatia, Slovenia, Bosnia-Herzegovina, Macedonia, Montenegro, and Serbia—have suffered through a long history of territorial fighting and boundary shifting.

Still, brave leaders did emerge. They believed the Balkan people should be allied against a common enemy. One of those leaders was the Serbian ruler Lazar Hrebeljanovic. In 1388 he struck an alliance with rulers in Bosnia and nearby Bulgaria, which is not considered a Balkan state but, nevertheless, had much to fear from the advancing Turkish army.

The alliance met the Turks in battle near Plocnik, a city in Serbia. The combined armies of the three nations defeated the Turks, and for a brief time it appeared as though the invaders would be forced to return to the Middle East. But the Ottoman army regrouped. Meanwhile, Bulgarian king Ivan Shishman sold out his Serbian and Bosnian allies, striking a deal with Murat I, the Ottoman sultan. That left the eastern front of Serbia unprotected. The Turks swarmed across the border, meeting the Serbs on a battlefield in the Serbian province of Kosovo known as the "Field of Blackbirds."

On the eve of the battle, the Serbs learned that they had been betrayed by the Bosnians as well and would have to face the Turks alone. Just as the two sides were about to clash, the Turks sent an emissary to Lazar offering to spare his life and the lives of his soldiers if the Serbs surrendered and agreed to Turkish rule of their nation. The Serbs were greatly outnumbered; to engage in battle against the Turks meant certain death. According to Serbian legend, a saint appeared to Lazar with a message from the Mother of God.

"What kingdom shall I choose?" Lazar is said to have asked himself. "Shall I choose a heavenly kingdom? Shall I choose an earthly kingdom? If I choose an earthly kingdom, an earthly kingdom lasts only a little time. But a heavenly kingdom will last for eternity."

Lazar chose the heavenly kingdom. The next morning he led his outnumbered Serbs against the Turks. The Serbs fought bravely. In fact, Murat was killed in the battle by Serbian hero Milos Obilic. But the Turks soon overran the Serbian defenders, pushed them aside, and conquered the Balkans. It would be more than 500 years before the Ottoman Turks released their grip on the Balkans.

In Serbia, Lazar is regarded with the same reverence as Abraham Lincoln in America. Not only did Lazar show courage in the face of an overwhelming enemy, but he did so against the reviled Turks: invaders who practiced the Muslim faith, they had long been regarded in Europe as a threat to Christianity.

"Beside the name of Christ, no other name is more beautiful or more sacred," Bishop Emilijan, a leader of the Serbian Orthodox church, said of Lazar at a ceremony in 1939 commemorating an anniversary of the battle.

Whatever else the battle on the Field of Blackbirds may teach about the Balkans, it certainly shows that the region has suffered through a long and terrible history of warfare, conquest, and betrayal. Indeed, the contentious history of the Balkans did not start with the betrayal of Lazar by the Bulgarians and Bosnians. By Lazar's time, the inhabitants of the Balkans had already spent centuries mistrusting one another, fleeing from one another's armies while making and breaking treaties with each other's allies and enemies.

The Balkans are composed of six states—Croatia, Slovenia, Bosnia-Herzegovina, Macedonia, Montenegro, and Serbia. Serbia is the largest and most populous of the states, and includes two autonomous regions—Kosovo and Vojvodina. The states are located along the eastern coast of the Adriatic Sea. Their southern neighbors are Albania and Greece; along the east, they are bordered by Bulgaria and Romania. Hungary, Austria, and Italy lie to the north.

Every year on June 28, citizens of the former Yugoslavia celebrate the battle of The Field of Blackbirds and the heroism of Serb King Lazar. On that day in 1389, Lazar fought and lost a battle against the Ottoman Turks, which led to 500 years of Ottoman Turk control of the region. In 1987, Serb president Slobodan Milosevic used the anniversary to conjure up the feverish Serb nationalism that led to division of Yugoslavia into five separate countries.

The original citizens of the Balkans were Slavic people who made their way south from Poland to escape invading German armies in the fifth century. At the time, the Slavs did not consider themselves fighters; they were farmers who sought only rich pastoral land to raise their livestock and grow crops in peace. They found it in the Balkans. Although certainly a mountainous area—the region is named for the Balkan Mountains—most of the land in the Balkans turned out to be fertile and tillable. The Slavs were able to plant grain fields, fruit orchards, and vineyards.

Over time, the cultures of the southern Slavic people evolved. What had been a common language evolved into many dialects. Slovenes and Macedonians developed their own languages. The other people of the Balkans spoke Serbo-Croatian, although Serbs and Croats use different alphabets.

Ruling families evolved as well. Powerful leaders emerged through warfare and conquest. Treaties were made and broken. Alliances were kept for only as long as they suited the ambitions of the rulers. Such squabbles among the ruling families of the Balkans persisted into the 20th century.

The Serbs were particularly plagued by intrigue, jealousy, and duplicity among their leaders. In 1815 the wealthy Karadjordjevic and Obrenovic families struck an alliance, raised an army, and led a successful uprising against the Turks. As a result of the alliance, Alexander Karadjordjevic was recognized as prince of Serbia; he lasted just a few years, and was replaced by Milos Obrenovic. The two families bitterly traded the throne back and forth for nearly a century. Often, the throne became vacant through assassination. At other times, bad decisions caused the downfall of the royals.

In 1865, Serbia was led by Michael Obrenovic, who could have been one of that country's greatest leaders. Michael saw the old ways changing—America, a country based on democracy, had just survived a civil war because of the strength of its principles. In western Europe kings were reluctantly giving up some of their power to parliaments. Michael agreed to share power with a Serbian Parliament and rule under the laws of a constitution. The Serbs still had much to fear from the Turks, and Michael made overtures to the other Balkan leaders to unite against their common enemy. Although the Serbs had succeeded in keeping the Turks at bay, the Ottomans were still occupying other Balkan states and posing a threat elsewhere in Europe. Alas, while forging the alliance Michael Obrenovic was assassinated.

Power shifted to his cousin Milan, who had little interest in parliaments and constitutions. Instead, Milan signed an ill-advised treaty with Austria-Hungary, which angered the Russians—fellow Slavs who regarded themselves as protectors of the Balkans. Next, Milan—fearing that the Bulgarians were planning to attack Macedonia—waged war on Bulgaria. Milan hoped the Russians would be drawn into the battle to protect the Bulgarians, and that Austria-Hungary would join the war on the side of the Serbs. But the war against Bulgaria was brief; none of the other major European powers participated, and the Serbs suffered a terrible defeat. Milan abdicated in 1889.

Milan was replaced by his son, Alexander. He ruled until 1903, when he was assassinated in a coup staged by the army. He was replaced by Peter Karadjordjevic.

The new king was a great admirer of Stefan Dusan, a Serbian ruler who served during the 12th century. Through an iron will and courage on the battlefield, Dusan extended the Serbian nation across a territory that included portions

Peter I, King of Serbia from 1903-1921, believed that Serbia could be returned to its former status as an eastern European empire. He led Bosnia and Herzegovina in a rebellion against Turkey.

of modern Greece, Macedonia, Albania, Montenegro, and Bosnia, as well as Serbia itself. Indeed, Stefan proclaimed himself emperor of the Balkans.

Peter Karadjordjevic was very much influenced by the nationalistic military leaders of Serbia who had, after all, murdered Alexander Obrenovic so that Peter could take the throne. Peter and his Serbian army sponsors believed that Serbia could return to its premier place as an eastern European empire, as it had been under Stefan Dusan. What's more, by the early 1900s the influence and power of the Ottoman Turks was very much on the wane. The once-powerful Turkish empire was now regarded as the "Sick Man of Europe." The empire suffered from poverty at home, poor training for soldiers, and laziness by their leaders, who were more interested in fattening their own fortunes than in defending the Ottomans' vast foreign holdings. In addition, the sultans had to contend with revolution in their capital of Constantinople. During the first years of the 20th century, the powers of the Ottoman sultans had eroded to the point where they no longer could count on the loyalty of their troops.

And so in Serbia, Karadjordjevic and other leaders spoke in favor of a fierce nationalism—a belief that Serbs should rule the Balkans. Karadjordjevic built up the Serbian army and gave military officers a hand in running the country. Little money was left over in the government's treasury for the needs of the people, but this matter seemed of little importance to the military rulers of the country. They insisted on more guns and forced the Serbian taxpayers to fund the expansion of the army. When the poor Serbian taxpayers could afford no more, the leaders turned to other countries to advance them loans. By 1906, the Serbs were in debt to the French for nearly 400 million francs.

In 1912, Serbia finally made its move. On October 8, Serbia and Montenegro declared war on the Turks. They were joined by the Greeks and Bulgarians, who saw the war as their chance to finally rid themselves of the Ottomans. Known as the First Balkan War, the conflict lasted just six weeks and resulted in a sweeping win for the Balkan states.

The victors were summoned to London by the English, French, and other European powers, who dictated the terms of a peace treaty that angered Serbia and Montenegro. The European powers decided that territory along the Adriatic Sea just below Montenegro would be created into the independent nation of Albania, which would be populated largely by people who had converted to Islam during the centuries of Turkish rule. As such, the territory would not become part of Serbia's desired empire of southern Slavs. The Serbs seethed over the terms of the Treaty of London. For centuries the Serbs had been forced to live side by side with a Muslim population in Kosovo, and they had been ill at ease in doing so.

The Treaty of London did not end the fighting. In June 1913, the Bulgarians launched attacks on the Serbs and Greeks in what became known as the Second Balkan War. The Bulgarians believed they had been cheated out of Ottoman territory in Macedonia that the Treaty of London awarded to Serbia. The attack was unwise. The Serbs and Greeks were joined by the Montenegrins in repelling the Bulgarian attack. The Romanians participated as well, and the allies were even joined by the Turks.

It was a bloody war. Neither side took prisoners, instead preferring to inflict terrible pain and suffering on their enemies. A Russian news correspondent, Vladimir Nemirovich-Danchenko, wrote about what he saw while visiting Karaj-Chiftlik, a Bulgarian village destroyed in a battle:

The closer we get, the more uneasy my guide and I become. Slaughtered cows. One mooing mournfully while trying to stand . . . We hear a ghastly scream. The guide clutches his rifle . . . The dead inhabit every house I enter . . . The church is completely blackened by fire. . . . Once my eyes get used to the dark, I see the pile of burnt bodies of people desperate to break down the doors, locked from the outside, as the building went up in flames.

Once the Bulgarians were defeated, the Balkan states turned against their old enemy, the Turks. Prince Alexander Karadjordjevic of Serbia crushed a concentration of Turkish troops in Macedonia. Elsewhere, Balkan armies attacked the Turks in Montenegro and Kosovo. Even the Bulgarians became allies against the Turks. In the Serbian capital of Belgrade, newspapers proclaimed the return of the "Old Serbia." The leaders of the Serbian government and military were now certain that they were on the verge of fulfilling their destiny of forging an empire of the southern Slavic people.

"Belgrade has a special air to it—on the alert like a military camp," wrote Russian journalist Leon Trotsky, who would later lead a revolution of his own in Russia.

Everyone and everything is subordinated to the demands of the mobilization . . . The streets are full of mobilized men and men about to be mobilized. The shops are empty . . . Industry is at a standstill, apart from the branch that serves the needs of mobilization and the coming war . . . For ten days already railway travel has been suspended in Serbia: the trains carry only soldiers and war materials . . . If Belgrade is an armed camp, the railway station is the heart of this camp. Military authority reigns there exclusively.

Russian Revolutionary Leon Trotsky, later a leader of the Russian Revolution, observed the military crackdown in Belgrade, describing the entire city as "on alert, like a military camp."

The Second Balkan War ended in August 1913. The costs of the two wars were high: more than 200,000 soldiers were killed. Thousands of civilians lost their lives to atrocities committed by the armies as well as to the disease of cholera, which swept through the war-torn lands. The fighting was waged over a front that stretched some 400 miles, from the Greek region of Thessaly in the south to the far border of Macedonia to the north. The Turks and Bulgarians were the big losers in the war: the Turks' influence in Europe was now all but over; as for the Bulgarians, more than 3,000 square miles of their nation were chopped up and distributed to the victors.

And amazingly enough, the carnage was not over. Indeed, it was just beginning.

In October 1912 a thin, pale young man from Bosnia made his way to the town of Prokuplje in Serbia and volunteered for the military service. The Serbian army had been amassing in Prokuplje, preparing for an attack on Turkish strongholds in Albania. The volunteer, Gavrilo Princip, had been inspired to join the Serbian army by the nationalistic rhetoric of the Serbian leaders. Although born a Bosnian, he believed there should be a southern Slavic empire and that it should be ruled by the Serbs.

Princip found the recruiting officer in Prokuplje and offered his services. But the officer, Major Vojin Tankosic, looked Princip up and down and declared him unfit for the rigors of battle ahead. "You are too small and too weak," he laughed.

Humiliated, Princip left Prokuplje and traveled to the Bosnian capital of Sarajevo. Still determined to serve the cause of a Serbian empire, Princip joined the Serbian Black Hand Society, a secret organization committed to the use of terrorism.

For Princip and other virulently nationalistic Slavs, there was one piece of unfinished business left over from the 19th century. In 1878, Russia defeated the Turks in a border skirmish and mobilized its army with the intention of seizing all Ottoman territory in Europe. Austria-Hungary intervened to halt the Russian advance. At the Congress of Berlin, which settled the issue of Russian expansion, Austria-Hungary was awarded possession of the former Ottoman lands in Bosnia-Herzegovina as well as in other Balkan states.

The Bosnians endured life under Austria-Hungary as bitterly as they had under the Turks. Elsewhere in the Balkans, the Slavs could do little about the Austria-Hungary occupation. Unlike the Turks, the dual monarchy of Austria-Hungary was in command of a powerful military force and, certainly, the relatively small armies of the Balkan states were no match for it.

Meeting secretly in Sarajevo, the Serbian Black Hand Society decided to take steps that the Bosnian government could not. Six members of the group, including Princip, lined up along a Sarajevo street known as Appel Quay on June 28, 1914. Each man was armed. Their intention was to assassinate Archduke Franz Ferdinand, son of Franz Joseph, the emperor of Austria-Hungary. The archduke was visiting Sarajevo that day, and his car was due to travel down Appel Quay. Ironically, Princip had been given his gun by Vojin Tankosic, the Serb army officer who had laughed him out of Prokuplje just two years before.

The car approached. Four of the conspirators could not find the courage and failed to draw their weapons. One conspirator, Nedeljko Cabrinovic, tossed a bomb that missed the archduke's car; it exploded in the crowd lining Appel Quay, injuring bystanders.

Archduke Franz Ferdinand walking to his car with his wife Sophie minutes before his assassination on June 28, 1914. The assassin, Gavrilo Princip fired two shots, killing both Franz and Sophie. The assassinations set off a chain reaction of events that eventually led to World War I.

Gavrilo Princip drew his gun and fired twice; the first shot hit the archduke, the second his wife, Sophie. Princip's shot struck Franz Ferdinand in the neck. "It is nothing. It is nothing," the wounded archduke told his bodyguards as they rushed to his side. He was dead within minutes. Sophie died as well.

Princip's shot did nothing less than touch off World War I.

Believing the government of Serbia was behind the assassination, Austria-Hungary declared war on the Balkan state. Russia entered the war on the side of the Serbs. Germany sided with Austria-Hungary. France opposed Germany. When Germany prepared to march through Belgium to attack France, the Belgians protested, claiming neutrality. The British warned the Germans not to violate Belgium's neutrality. When German troops flooded across the Belgian border, the British entered the war. By the time it was over in 1918, virtually every nation in the Western Hemisphere—including the United States—would be at war.

The Balkan nation that emerged from the rubble of World War I was close to the Serbs' prewar dream of a united south Slavic empire. Following the defeat of Germany and the other Central Powers, Balkan leaders agreed to the Corfu Declaration, named for the Greek island on which it was negotiated. The declaration outlined the structure of a future southern Slav nation, to be composed of Serbia, Croatia, and Slovenia. The new country, the Kingdom of the Serbs, Croats, and Slovenes, was formed on December 1, 1918. Vojvodina, Montenegro, and Bosnia-Herzegovina joined the new union as well. Serbian prince Alexander Karadjordjevic, hero of the Second Balkan War, was named king. A parliament would run the government.

At last it appeared the Serbs finally had what they wanted—a unified kingdom of southern Slavic people under their control. But social and economic conditions in Europe following World War I hardly gave the Serbs much of an opportunity to build their new kingdom into an empire. Anarchism swept through Europe. The new kingdom was not immune to the lawlessness. The Croats, in particular, agitated to break away from the kingdom; in 1928, Croatian leader Stjepan Radic was assassinated by a Montenegrin. In response, the Croats announced their independence and the establishment of their own government in the city of Zagreb. Civil war seemed imminent. King Alexander stepped in and abolished the Parliament. Hoping to unite the nation and avoid civil war, Alexander wiped out provincial borders and renamed the country Yugoslavia. In the Slavic language, "yugo" means south.

Nobody seemed happy with the king's decision, and indeed, in 1934 Alexander paid for it with his life. Like so many of his predecessors, Alexander was assassinated.

Tensions were building elsewhere in Europe. In Russia, the Bolsheviks came to power, installing a communist regime. In Germany, Adolf Hitler and the Nazis promised to rebuild their country into a mighty fighting machine. By 1939, the world was at war again. Yugoslavia was invaded by Germans, who once again partitioned the country. Parts of Yugoslavia were turned over to the Italians, who were allies of the Germans. Croatian fascists known as the Ustashi were given a free hand by the Germans to murder their enemies. Jews, Muslims, and Serbs felt the brunt of the Ustashi wrath. For the Yugoslavs, the years under German and Ustashi domination in World War II were a brutal and bloody period. During the war, 1.7 million

Yugoslavs died—more than a million of them killed by other Yugoslavs.

In the mountains, resistance fighters known as the "Partisans" held out. They were led by a Croatian communist, Josep Broz, who was known to his followers as Tito. When the war ended in 1945, Tito emerged as an immensely popular leader and would, in fact, lead the government of Yugoslavia for the next 35 years. Unlike the Soviet Union, which was forever plagued with a poor economy, Tito made communism work. He was able to establish healthy industries, farms that produced enough food for his people, and modern cities featuring skyscrapers and efficient transportation networks. During his reign the Yugoslavian military was strong and united. By the force of his personality as well as an iron will and a desire to use the state to oppress opposition, Tito was able to accomplish what no southern Slav had been able to do since Stefan Dusan forged a Serbian empire in the 12th century. He brought together the diverse ethnic groups of Yugoslavia into a peaceful coexistence.

But in 1980, Tito died.

Nearly a decade later, a Serb named Slobodan Milosevic came to power in Yugoslavia. In one of his first major speeches, Milosevic recalled how Lazar and his men had gone to their deaths in defense of Serbia.

"After six centuries we are again waging struggle and confronting battles," he told a crowd of some 2 million Serbs. "These are not armed struggles, though that cannot yet be excluded."

Milosevic told the Serbian people that it was their destiny to rule over a southern Slav empire.

He made that promise to them in a speech delivered on the Field of Blackbirds.

TITO

Like many people in Yugoslavia, Josep Broz found himself growing up with divided loyalties. And yet, he would find a way to overcome centuries of hate and suspicion in the Balkans to forge a united Yugoslavia.

Born in 1892, he was the son of a Slovenian mother and Croatian father who owned a farm near the village of Kumrovec, a region of Croatia awarded to Austria-Hungary in an 1878 treaty. His father had hoped to send Josep to America to study, but lacked the money for his passage and tuition. Instead, Josep studied metalworking and locksmithing. While learning his trade, he joined the metalworkers union and adopted its socialist ideas.

In 1913, at the age of 21, he was drafted into the army of Austria-Hungary. In 1915, while fighting in Russia during World War I, he was wounded and captured by the Russian army. Broz remained in Russia as a prisoner of war until 1917, when Tsar Nicholas was deposed by the Bolsheviks. As a socialist, his sympathies were clearly with the Bolsheviks. He joined the Bolsheviks and fought alongside them during the civil war that followed their takeover of the Russian government.

Following the civil war he returned to Zagreb in Croatia, where he organized a communist party in what was now the Kingdom of the Serbs, Croats, and Slovenes. The government of King Alexander Karadjordjevic feared the communists, believing they could spark a revolution as they had done in Russia. He had Broz thrown in jail.

Later, Broz expressed no hostility toward Karadjordjevic for imprisoning him.

"It was only natural that when they caught me they should shut me up," he said. "I would have done the same thing in their place."

He was released in 1934. He spent three years in Moscow, rising in rank among communist leaders. When he returned to Yugoslavia in 1937, he was known as "Tito," a common nickname from his old Croatian village.

When World War II reached Yugoslavia in 1941, the country was invaded by the Germans, who turned the government over to

Croatian fascists known as the Ustashi. The communists became targets of Ustashi terror; Tito was forced to hide in the mountains, where he organized resistance fighters known as the Partisans. Under Tito, the Partisans fought hard, sacrificing their lives to drive the Nazis from their land. In 1943, when Italy surrendered, the Partisans captured an enormous store of Italian arms, giving them an upper hand in their mountain battles. By 1944, Tito was regarded as one of the heroes of the war and included in discussions by the Allied leaders on their future plans for Europe once the war ended. In 1945, he was named prime minister of Yugoslavia.

Tito was a communist and looked to the Soviet Union for leadership. The friendship was short-lived. During his dealings with Soviet leader Joseph Stalin, it soon became clear to Tito that the Soviets wanted to exploit Yugoslavia's vast reserves of ore and other natural resources. On June 28, 1948, Tito announced Yugoslavia had broken relations with the Soviet Union. The Soviets threatened to invade Yugoslavia, but backed off when the United States said it would protect the smaller nation. Over the years, communist leaders made overtures to Tito to bring his nation back into the Soviet bloc, but Tito always refused. On the other hand, he refused to accept Western investment and human rights reforms, choosing instead to steer a course of neutrality.

In the meantime, he made communism work for the people of Yugoslavia, using Yugoslavian materials and laborers to build cities, highways, and industries. Although Yugoslavs occasionally had to endure cold winters and empty store shelves, they were far better off than their fellow communists in the Soviet Union. And because he was such a powerful leader, Tito would not tolerate the petty jealousies and suspicions that had divided the Yugoslavian people for 1,000 years. He died in 1980 after providing for the revolving presidency that he was sure would continue to rule Yugoslavia in peace long after he was gone.

3

Little Lenin

When thousands of international visitors streamed into Sarajevo for the 1984 Winter Olympics, they were greeted by the toothy image of "Vucko," the official cartoon mascot for the games. Vucko, the little wolf, was picked by the people of the Bosnian city to display a message of friendship to the visitors.

The athletes put on valiant performances. In Alpine skiing, Americans Phil Mahre, Bill Johnson, and Debbie Armstrong won gold medals. The United States also scored a gold medal in men's figure skating when Scott Hamilton finished first in his competition. Among the star performers from other countries were East German Katarina Witt, winner of the gold in women's figure skating, and Jayne Torvoll and Christopher Dean, champion ice dancers from Great Britain. Finally, the ice hockey team from the Soviet Union avenged its 1980 upset loss to the Americans by winning the gold medal at the Sarajevo Olympics.

More than 1,500 athletes from 49 countries participated in the Winter Olympics in 1984. Except for a blizzard that

The opening ceremonies of the 1984 Winter Olympics were held in Sarajevo's Kosovo stadium. The games ran smoothly, even while extremist groups were gaining power and influence throughout Yugoslavia.

temporarily delayed some of the skiing events, the games ran smoothly. Sarajevo officials were particularly delighted that the competitions were held in the Bosnian city during a peaceful time in Yugoslavia, free of the protest and political activism that had often marred Olympic competitions in the past.

That may have been true for the 12 days of the Sarajevo Olympics, but elsewhere in the country, sinister forces were at work. Indeed, dark times were ahead for Yugoslavia and its people.

While fans gathered in Sarajevo to watch ice hockey games, bobsled races, and Alpine skiers race down mountainsides, Slobodan Milosevic was hard at work in nearby Belgrade running the city's Communist Party. He was the protégé of Ivan Stambolic, a rising political force in Yugoslavia. In 1984, when Stambolic became Communist Party chief of Serbia, he picked Milosevic to head the organization in the republic's largest city.

During the height of communist power in the former Soviet Union and the other Eastern European nations, the Communist Party chief wielded considerable power. In America and other democratic nations, political party leaders help pick candidates for office and run their campaigns, but they have no role in the government once the election is over. In the dictatorships of the former communist era, there were no free elections. The Communist Party chiefs selected candidates who were expected to do their bidding once they assumed office. For Yugoslavian communists, the job of party chief in Belgrade was a tremendously important position. Belgrade was not only the capital of Serbia but also of the entire nation of Yugoslavia. Every job Milosevic carried out would be under the close scrutiny of the nation's most powerful leaders.

Milosevic was born on August 22, 1941, in Pozarevac, a small town east of Belgrade. Although he would grow up among Serbs, promising his people that he would lead them in creation of a south Slavic empire, Milosevic was not a Serb himself. His parents, Svetozar and Stanislava Milosevic, were Montenegrins who fled to Pozarevac the year before

Slobodan's birth to escape the onslaught of Nazi troops. They weren't safe in Pozarevac for long. Soon, the German army would sweep through the entire nation of Yugoslavia, inflicting tremendous terror on the Slavic people.

The Milosevics survived the war and the years of poverty and hunger that followed the defeat of the German army. Slobodan grew up with barely enough food to eat and clothes to cover his body. In America in the late 1940s and early 1950s, families were enjoying the availability of such modern appliances as washers and dryers, refrigerators, televisions, and electric ranges. In Yugoslavia, fathers chopped firewood to provide heat and mothers laundered their families' clothes with washboards at the river's edge.

Conditions would improve. Under Tito, the roads were slowly rebuilt, cities rose from the ashes, and farms started producing food again. There was no question that Tito was a communist—he ruled the country with an iron will, suppressed freedoms, jailed opponents, and restricted personal freedoms, but conditions were much worse under the Soviets as well as their puppet leaders in Romania, Poland, East Germany, and other satellite nations. In Yugoslavia, the communist system was hailed as the savior of life, and all young Yugoslavs soon realized that if they expected to obtain an important job with a good salary, they would do well to become committed communists.

Slobodan Milosevic was a committed communist. In fact, he was such an enthusiast for the party system that his schoolmates started calling him "Little Lenin," a nickname honoring the communist founder of the Soviet Union, Vladimir Lenin.

Milosevic was also a bright student. By 1960 he was attending law school in Belgrade, where he met and made friends with another law student, Ivan Stambolic. Even as students, the two young men quickly rose up through the

After meeting in law school, Slobodan Milosevic and Ivan Stambolic quickly moved up the political ladder. As head of the Serbian Communist Party, Stambolic appointed Milosevic party leader. Milosevic lead Yugoslavia to poverty, repeated military defeats and made Yugoslavia universally hated. He was the first former head of a nation indicted by the U.N. war crimes tribunal.

ranks of the communist hierarchy. For Ivan, he had his uncle Petar to thank for his rise in power. Petar Stambolic was a top Communist Party official in Yugoslavia; clearly, Ivan's family connections would help pave his way to a position of leadership.

Milosevic had no important family connections and, in fact, may have had to overcome suspicions about his fiancée's commitment to the communist cause. Milosevic was engaged to Mira Markovic, whose mother, Vera Miletic, was a spy and saboteur working for Tito's Partisans during World War II. Vera Miletic regarded herself as a devoted communist, but during the war she was captured by the Nazis, tortured, and executed. After her death the Nazis rounded up a number of the Partisans, dragging them from their homes and executing them in the streets. It was believed that Vera succumbed to torture and gave the Nazis the names of her comrades. For years, Mira had to endure talk among Yugoslavs that her mother had been a coward.

Mira and Slobodan overcame such talk by committing themselves to communism. While at law school, Milosevic first came to the attention of Communist Party officials during a debate on a proposal by Tito to change the name of the country. Forever feuding with communists in the Soviet Union, Tito had decided to drop the phrase "People's Republic" from the official name of the country. The term had been coined by Joseph Stalin, the World War II-era Soviet leader whom Tito had long hated. Instead of the "People's Republic of Yugoslavia," Tito favored "Federal Socialist Republic of Yugoslavia." He asked universities to hold forums on the name change; one such forum was held in 1963 at the University of Belgrade, which was attended by 22-year-old law student Slobodan Milosevic. During the debate on the name, Milosevic rose from his seat and made one simple suggestion: in naming a communist state, the word "socialist" should have the most emphasis. Therefore, he said, the name of the country should be the "Socialist Federal Republic of Yugoslavia."

The hard-line communists sitting on the stage approved Milosevic's idea. The young law student was now responsible for having a hand in the name of his country. In Belgrade, Milosevic's star was beginning to rise. After graduating from law school, he was made an aide to the mayor of Belgrade and slowly started ascending the ladder of power in the Yugoslavian communist system. In 1965 he married Mira and soon after declared his nationality Serbian, giving up his Montenegrin citizenship.

In 1968 he was given the important job of head of information in the Belgrade city government. This was one of the most important positions in the city communist structure. In communist countries, there is no free press—the newspapers, television, and radio stations are controlled by the Communist Party—meaning the people read and hear the news that the local party chiefs think people should read and hear. As head of information in the country's largest city, Milosevic had control over the nation's largest newspapers and other media outlets.

That year, Mira and her cousin were strolling down a Belgrade street when the two women stopped in front of a shop window, where they saw Tito's photograph displayed.

"One day Slobo's photograph will also be there," Mira told her cousin.

"What do you mean?" the cousin said. "You think Slobo will be president of Serbia?"

Mira answered: "Slobo's picture, like Tito's, will be displayed in shop windows."

Stambolic was rising as well in the Communist Party. Together, the two men seemed to have a bright future ahead of them in Tito's system.

But Tito died in 1980. The 87-year-old communist led the country for nearly four decades. Before he died, Tito devised a system of succession that he thought would hold the country's diverse nationalities together: the presidency would change hands every year for the next eight years, to be held by the leaders of the six republics and two autonomous regions. For a nation that had endured 1,000 years of suspicion and betrayal, the system soon proved unworkable. Soon, old rivalries emerged and the fatherly, mythical figure of Tito was no longer standing tall over the land to ease the tensions. The people who were upset the most at the new order were the Serbs; they made up two-thirds of the Yugoslavian population. Why did they have to share power equally with the Croats or, even worse, the Muslim Kosovars?

Milosevic realized the old order was crumbling. By 1986 he was Communist Party leader of Serbia. In Kosovo, ethnic Serbs were complaining about their treatment under the rule of the party's Muslim majority. Ivan Stambolic, now the president of Serbia, dispatched Milosevic to Kosovo to ease the tensions. "Calm them down," he told Milosevic.

When the Communist Party chief arrived in Kosovo, he was met by an angry crowd of Serbs with a long list of grievances. Many Serbs complained that the Kosovo police had been roughing them up. Shocked by the treatment of Serbs, Milosevic suddenly blurted out: "No one will ever dare beat you again!"

The crowd responded to Milosevic's promise. Soon, they were applauding Milosevic and shouting his name: "Slobo! Slobo!"

He continued:

> You must stay here. Your land is here. Here are your houses, your fields and gardens, your memories. You are not going to leave them, are you, because life is hard and because you are subjected to injustice and humiliation? It was never in the spirit of the Serb and Montenegrin peoples to succumb before obstacles, to quit when one has to fight, to be demoralized in the face of hardship.

Under Tito, such incendiary language from a party leader would have been unthinkable. For the 35 years of his reign, Tito demanded Yugoslavian unity, but now Milosevic had told the Serbian people that he was on their side, that they would not have to endure the struggle against the Kosovars alone.

Slavko Curuvija, a journalist who covered the speech for his newspaper that day, said: "He instantly became the leader of all Serbs."

While Milosevic was first to realize that things were changing inside Yugoslavia, he was also among the first of the communist leaders to see that the end was near for communism as a way of life in the Soviet Union and the countries of Eastern Europe. In the Soviet Union, decades of leadership by hard-line communists ended in 1985 when Mikhail Gorbachev became general secretary of the Communist Party—the most powerful position in the vast country. Gorbachev took over during a period of deep economic trouble for the Soviet Union: farmers and factories were failing to produce, and the Soviet people were forced to stand in long lines to buy food and other simple necessities of life. Unlike his predecessors, Gorbachev realized that the Soviets would have to adopt Western-style principles of business and open their country's borders to international investment in order to avoid a complete economic collapse. Under his policy of "glasnost"—which meant "openness"—he granted the Soviet people more personal freedoms, encouraged American corporations to do business in the Soviet Union (this was the era when McDonald's opened a restaurant in Moscow's Bolshoi Square), and made over-tures to President Ronald Reagan to cease the nuclear arms race that had existed between the two countries since the end of World War II. For communists, the end finally came in 1991. Despite Gorbachev's reforms, the economy of the Soviet Union continued to deteriorate.

Former Soviet President Mikhail Gorbachev introduced reforms such as Glasnost and Perestroika that opened up the Soviet Union to western business and political reform. Slobodan Milosevic recognized early on that Yugoslavia would have to adapt to the collapse of Communism in Eastern Europe.

Hard-line communists believed a return to the restrictive life of the past would help turn the country around. They staged a coup d'état against Gorbachev; the Soviet leader was arrested and the hard-liners announced they were now in control of the country. But the military and the people stayed loyal to Boris Yeltsin, the communist leader of the Russian republic; he put down the coup and freed Gorbachev. Nevertheless, Yeltsin made it clear that communism was now dead. He forced Gorbachev to step down as general secretary and, together with the leaders of the other former Soviet republics, presided over the breakup of the Union of Soviet Socialist Republics that had been forged by Vladimir Lenin, Leon Trotsky, Joseph Stalin, and the other communist leaders following the Bolshevik revolution of 1917.

The tidal wave against communism spread to the Eastern European countries that had long been under Soviet domination. Communist leaders in Poland, East Germany, Czechoslovakia, and Romania were booted out of office. Many were imprisoned, some executed. In Berlin, the wall that had divided the city's communist side from its free side since 1961 was torn down by jubilant Germans, who were finally freed of their communist oppressors.

In America and the other democratic nations, people turned on their televisions to watch the collapse of international communism and the end of the Cold War. They saw the Berlin Wall fall down, statues of Lenin toppled in Moscow, and a former shipyard worker named Lech Walesa who had been imprisoned under the communists take office as president of Poland. Americans were also preoccupied elsewhere: in August 1990, Iraqi soldiers crossed the border into neighboring Kuwait, declaring the tiny but oil-rich nation in the Middle East a part of the territory ruled over by the dictator Saddam Hussein. Soon, Americans and other western powers would storm into the deserts to fight back the Iraqi aggressors.

Few people in the free world noticed the first shots fired in Croatia.

By 1991 the Yugoslavia that Tito forged following World War II was on the verge of collapse. The rotating presidency had been unable to solve Yugoslavia's economic woes, which were not as deep as those suffered in the Soviet Union but, nevertheless, times were not prosperous. Buoyed by the breakup of the Soviet Union, Yugoslavia's republics sought autonomy as well.

In Slovenia, leaders of the republic's government announced plans to secede from the union. In Croatia, a government under the control of Franjo Tudjman came to power. Tudjman announced that Croatia also intended to secede from Yugoslavia.

Meanwhile, the Communist Party of Yugoslavia quickly disintegrated. In January 1990, delegates to a party convention bickered so much over the complaints of Slovenia and Croatia that communist leaders finally adjourned the meeting with the hopes that delegates could work out their differences and reconvene. The Communist Party was, after all, the final unifying authority over the six republics and two provinces of Yugoslavia.

Indeed, during the contentious convention the delegates couldn't even agree on which patriotic song to sing to open the meeting. Exasperated, delegate Ivica Racan of Croatia told the other communist leaders, "It is not important how we begin, but it is important to finish with Yugoslavia."

Alas, the delegates never reconvened their convention. Communism in Yugoslavia was now dead, as it was elsewhere in Eastern Europe.

In Yugoslavia, the calls for independence continued. In Croatia, the cauldron seemed to boil the hottest.

Ethnic Serbs made up just 12 percent of the Croatian

population. They had never forgotten the terror inflicted on them during World War II by the Croatian fascists known as the Ustashi. To Serbs, the idea of living under Croatian rule was unthinkable. And so, they demanded autonomy from the Croatian majority.

In Belgrade, Slobodan Milosevic continued to extend his power and influence. In 1989, he made his speech at the Field of Blackbirds in Kosovo, then wrested the Serbian presidency from his old friend Stambolic, who still believed in Tito's philosophy of unity. But Milosevic appealed instead to the fierce nationalism he knew burned deep inside every Serb, promising them their place at the head of a south Slavic empire.

With tensions heading to a boil in Croatia, Milosevic announced that if Croatia and other republics seceded from Yugoslavia, the Serbs would insist on redrawn borders so that ethnic Serbs in the former republics would be part of a new Serbian nation. In June 1991 Croatia and Slovenia declared their independence. The first shots were fired on June 25. Milosevic sent 2,000 Yugoslavian soldiers into Slovenia to put down the secession, but it was a half-hearted gesture. Secretly, Milosevic had already promised Slovenian president Milan Kucan that he would not oppose Slovenian independence; indeed, with just 6 percent of the country composed of ethnic Serbs, Milosevic had little to gain by forcing all-out war in Slovenia. Hostilities were over within 10 days; the death toll was recorded at less than 100—most of them soldiers in Milosevic's army.

The real war was still to come. That August, ethnic Serbs in Croatia started carrying out a guerrilla war against Croatian troops. They fought hard and soon had the upper hand against the Croats. And they were greatly aided by the Yugoslavian Air Force, which had been dispatched by

Milosevic. Meanwhile, Serbian paramilitary fighters, including Arkan's Tigers, made their way across the border and launched strikes on the Croats as well.

First to fall under attack was the Croatian town of Vukovar. Other cities also soon felt the brunt of the Serbian attack. And this war was unlike other wars—the two sides targeted more than just each other's soldiers. Civilians caught in the cross fire were shown no mercy. Hospitals were leveled by bombs. The paramilitary fighters had no qualms about harassing, arresting, and executing civilians.

The fighting was particularly hostile in Vukovar, where soldiers often found themselves engaging in hand-to-hand combat. For weeks, the Serbian attackers inched their way through the streets. Finally, the city fell on November 17. Vukovar was of strategic importance: by controlling the city, the Serbs had an open path across the narrow Croatian plain toward the republic's capital at Zagreb. Said Zivota Panic, the Serbian Army general in charge of the Vukovar offensive, "The moment Vukovar fell, Croatia lost the war."

Milosevic decided not to send troops further into Croatia. He declared that the offensive had met its goal—to protect the ethnic Serbs living in Croatia and lay the groundwork for the eventual takeover of the Serbian regions of the country.

"We could have marched easily on," said Panic. "But President Milosevic said, among other things, that we must stop. And that was the order from the defense minister and I just obeyed. We protected the Serb areas."

The Serbian aggression in Croatia was watched carefully by the citizens of Bosnia-Herzegovina. Bosnia had a Serbian minority that ached to be free of the country's ethnic Muslim leadership.

Vukovar was the sight of the fiercest fighting in Croatia's battle for secession. After Serbian soldiers finally took Vukovar, Croatia gained both international support and sympathy.

In March 1992 Bosnia-Herzegovina announced that it would follow Croatia and Slovenia and secede from Yugoslavia. The Serbian minority reacted quickly, arming themselves and setting up roadblocks around Bosnian cities. The Tigers and other paramilitary units flooded across the borders.

Within a short time Macedonia would secede from Yugoslavia as well, leaving only Serbia and Montenegro and two autonomous provinces—Kosovo and Vojvodina —members of what had been Tito's Yugoslavia.

And in the Bosnian city of Sarajevo, where Vucko the little wolf had welcomed Olympic visitors with a broad toothy smile just eight years before, people went about their lives, unaware of the horror that awaited them.

4

Sarajevo

For nearly two years, the citizens of Sarajevo endured constant pummeling by mortar fire, sniper attacks, raids on their homes by paramilitary thugs, as well as hunger caused by a complete blockade of their city by the Bosnian Serbs. But on August 28, 1994, they suffered an atrocity that would shock the world and mark a turning point in the Bosnian war.

Just past noon in Sarajevo's Market Square, hundreds of starving Sarajevans lined up for their daily ration of bread. More people than usual came out to the public square because on that bright, crisp day in Sarajevo, the war seemed to be taking the day off. There had been no shelling that morning, and people thought it would be safe to venture outdoors.

They were wrong.

Suddenly, a mortar shell exploded in Market Square. Sixty-nine people were killed waiting in line for bread. More than 200 people were injured.

"We Bosnians feel condemned to death," said Alija Izetbegovic, president of Bosnia-Herzegovina.

A bombed out building in Sarajevo is just one sign of the intense shelling that the city and people of Sarajevo had to endure for almost two years. "Welcome to Sarajevo" became a sad introduction to a once proud city.

The events leading up to the blockade and assault on the city commenced in November 1991 when Bosnian Serbs declared their independence from Bosnia-Herzegovina. Bosnia's population as well as its government were dominated by a Muslim majority, but there was a significant population of Serbs and Croats within the republic's borders.

The rebellious Bosnian Serbs were led by Radovan Karadzic, a university psychologist, poet, and vicious racist whose independence movement was encouraged by Milosevic in Belgrade. Secretly, Karadzic started organizing a Bosnian Serb army. He was helped by Milosevic, who provided officers, arms, and equipment from the Yugoslavian army. By early 1992, Karadzic found himself at the head of a force of some 90,000 Bosnian Serb soldiers.

The official Bosnia-Herzegovina government in Sarajevo never recognized the independence of the Bosnian Serbs. In March, voters in the republic approved their own referendum calling for secession from what was left of the Yugoslavian federation. As expected, the Bosnian Serbs reacted bitterly to the vote; they immediately took up arms and, assisted by the paramilitary groups from Serbia, surrounded the cities and set up roadblocks.

"We are not going to accept an independent Bosnia-Herzegovina," declared Karadzic. "Let this be a warning."

Karadzic insisted that Bosnian Serbs be given the right to national self-determination—that they be free to form their own republic along the Drina River just south of Sarajevo or remain part of the Yugoslavia ruled by Milosevic.

All the Bosnian cities except the capital of Sarajevo capitulated quickly. Foolishly, Sarajevans believed a display of peace and unity would turn away the Bosnian Serb onslaught. After all, Sarajevans had coexisted for generations; some 50 percent of all married Sarajevans were members of mixed marriages. Thousands of Sarajevans took to the streets to march for peace.

On the outskirts of the city, though, the Bosnian Serbs refused to yield. By the spring of 1992, the city was under constant mortar fire.

"The war in Bosnia-Herzegovina is what it is—pitiless, cruel, and savage," wrote Sarajevo journalist Zlatko

Dizdarevic on May 1, 1992. "Very often it lacks rational objectives, except for a fundamental and general one: conquering as much territory as possible to be annexed to the new state on the other side of the river Drina."

The attacks were relentless. Bosnian Serbs lobbed mortar shells into the city from their posts on the outskirts. Snipers would sneak into hiding places among the rubble, picking off human targets with single shots. It made no difference to the snipers whether their targets were civilian or military: schools, hospitals, newspaper offices, and food warehouses were all targets of the Bosnian Serb siege.

"I hated the snipers more than anything else," wrote American journalist Peter Maass.

> First you heard the crack of their shots, then the whistle of the bullet, then the echo of the crack and then silence. Everything happened in a millisecond. Crack, whistle, echo, silence. The sound was uniquely chilling, in a way that made it feel more menacing than a mortar blast or the rat-tat-tat of a machine gun. A sniper shoots one bullet at a time, a bullet that stands out as distinctly as a single, piercing note from an opera diva overpowering her chorus. You hear that lone shot and you know, instinctively, that the bullet is aimed at somebody, perhaps you.

In Belgrade, Milosevic pulled the strings of the Bosnian Serbs, but just as he had done the year before in Croatia, the Serbian ruler refused to commit his army to a full invasion.

There were many reasons for Milosevic's reluctance to use the overwhelming military might he held in his hand. By invading Bosnia-Herzegovina, he risked war with America and the other western nations. Now that Saddam's troops had been pushed back to Iraq, America turned its attention on the Balkan crisis. In Washington, former President George

A civilian runs for his life as he comes under sniper fire in Sarajevo. The snipers fired at anyone in their path and did not care if their targets were civilians or even children.

Bush recognized the independence of Bosnia-Herzegovina. He was prodded into extending diplomatic relations to the Izetbegovic government by Saudi Arabia and America's other allies in the Middle East, which were concerned about the extermination of fellow Muslims in Bosnia.

Meanwhile, Milosevic found his government broke and dealing with unrest at home. The previous year's wars in Croatia and Slovenia had been expensive—they bled dry the Yugoslavian treasury, leaving Milosevic no money to pay the government's employees. Overall, the economy was in a shambles. Inflation was running away, making the dinar—the national currency—virtually worthless. For the first time as president of Yugoslavia, Milosevic started hearing protests. University students flooded into the streets of Belgrade, demanding Milosevic's ouster.

To quiet the protesters, Milosevic appeared on Yugoslavian television to assure his people that the war in Bosnia-Herzegovina was being waged by Bosnian Serbs, and that Yugoslavia's mostly Serbian army had no hand in the fighting.

"Serbia is not at war," he declared. "Not a single soldier who is a citizen of the Republic of Serbia is outside Serbia's borders."

To the besieged people of Sarajevo, it didn't matter much to them whether the soldiers hurling grenades at their homes were Serbs from Serbia or Serbs from Bosnia. As the siege continued, the hardships of life in a war zone began to take their toll. Maass wrote of waking each morning in his hotel room and gazing down from his window at a park below, watching its transformation from a place of peace and beauty to an ugly stretch of bare earth.

He wrote:

> Before Bosnia went mad, the park was a pleasant place with wood benches and trees and neighborhood children playing tag on the grass. The war changed all that. The benches and trees vanished, scavenged for firewood. The stumps and roots were torn out, too—that's how cold and desperate people were in the winter. What remained was a denuded bit of earth that became an apocalyptic shooting gallery in which the ammunition was live, and so were the targets, until they got hit.

Meanwhile, food and water were scarce. The Bosnian Serbs had knocked out the power plants, so there was no electricity. Water stopped flowing through the city's pipes.

"For days there has been no running water," wrote Dizdarevic. "It rained yesterday, but many of us didn't think to collect the water in pots and buckets. How would we think of collecting rainwater, after so many years in which water ran from the tap? But the next time it rains, if it does, we'll know what to do."

Sarajevans found themselves risking their lives just to provide food for their families. Dizdarevic wrote of one amazing incident he learned about in a famine-stricken neighborhood of the city:

> One person managed to get up on the roof of the building in which the sniper had installed himself, and lowered a plastic bag containing a loaf of black bread past the side of the sniper's window down to the next level, where another person attached a rock to the end of the line and managed to throw it to a neighbor waiting behind an open window in the building across the way. As soon as this line had been made taut between the two buildings, probably to the astonishment of the sniper who must have been watching, the bread bag was slid down along the line. Witnesses said that at one point it got stuck on the branch of a tree, but unexpectedly a long pole appeared out of a nearby window and sent the loaf on its way again. Finally understanding what was going on, the sniper opened fire, hoping to hit the bag or the line or whatever he could, but by then it was too late: the loaf had reached the window it was destined for. Deafening applause, shouts of joy, and a few shots rang out from the surrounding buildings. This is the story of Sarajevo and its proud citizens who will bend neither their backs nor their heads.

And so the city fought on. Muslims were able to smuggle guns and ammunition into the besieged city so that the defenders could hold their ground. Diplomats from America, Great Britain, and other Western powers flew into the Balkan capitals, attempting to resolve the stalemate. An

Bosnian Serb leader Radovan Karadzic, in the midst of an assembly with parliamentary speaker Momcilo Krjisnik, kept up the relentless assault on Bosnia-Herzegovina even though its citizens were barely able to survive, struggling to simply clothe and feed themselves.

airlift of food, clothes, blankets, and other supplies was commenced by United Nations relief workers. The Sarajevo airport had long been closed, but it reopened under guard by United Nations peacekeeping troops.

The Western nations went a step further, imposing sanctions on the already strained economy of Yugoslavia. It meant that companies in America, Great Britain, and other major countries were forbidden from trading with the Balkan nation. Unable to obtain parts for their factories, seeds for their farms, and oil for their automobiles, Serbs found themselves struggling to feed and clothe themselves.

And yet, Milosevic refused to seek peace. Radovan Karadzic's troops kept up their relentless assault. By now, the Bosnian Serbs were in control of some 70 percent of the territory in Bosnia-Herzegovina, including all the major cities except Sarajevo. For the aggressors, it seemed as though it was just a matter of time until Sarajevo finally fell and with it, the government of President Izetbegovic.

And then came the Market Square bombing.

American diplomat Richard Holbrooke had been shuttling throughout the Balkan states as well as other European capitals in an effort to resolve the crisis. On the morning of August 28, 1994, he was in Paris, France, to confer with Izetbegovic in a meeting arranged by French diplomats. For months, Holbrooke had been warning the Bosnian Serbs that unless the siege ended, the powerful North Atlantic Treaty Organization would use its jets to strike against their positions. Now, in Paris, he turned on the television in his hotel room and watched news coverage of the Market Square massacre. Holbrooke realized it was finally time for NATO to strike.

"What counted was whether the United States would act decisively and persuade its NATO allies to join in the sort of massive air campaign that we had so often talked about but never even come close to undertaking," Holbrooke said. "Would our threats and warnings . . . finally be backed up with action?"

NATO is composed of the United States, Canada, Great Britain, France, and other European countries. The alliance formed in an effort to protect its members against the type of aggression that had sparked World War II. During the war, Great Britain had been attacked relentlessly by German bombers. America was drawn into the war by the Japanese attack on Pearl Harbor. Under the NATO treaty, if any single member of the alliance was attacked, NATO would regard that attack as an aggression against the entire alliance. Since NATO's formation in 1949, not a single member had been attacked by a hostile army.

Holbrooke knew it would take the might of NATO to

end the siege on Sarajevo. Soon, he found himself on the phone with Strobe Talbott, acting secretary of state. "I told him to start NATO air strikes against the Bosnian Serbs— not minor retaliatory 'pinpricks,' but a serious and, if possible, sustained air campaign."

NATO struck hard on August 30. The jets used their superior fire power to destroy the Bosnian Serb positions surrounding the city. The mortars and grenade launchers the Serbs had used to blast the roofs off hospitals and kill innocent civilians in public squares were no match for the sophisticated weaponry of the NATO fighter jets. What's more, NATO employed cruise missiles to wipe out the Bosnian Serb army command center at Banja Luka north of Sarajevo. During the attacks, not a single NATO jet was damaged by ground fire. The strikes delivered a devastating blow on the Bosnian Serbs, forcing them to retreat from the city. The Muslim and Croat defenders overran their positions. For the first time in 30 months, an uneasy but welcome peace hung over Sarajevo.

The Americans organized a peace conference at Wright-Patterson Air Force Base near Dayton, Ohio. Milosevic attended, as well as Alija Izetbegovic of Bosnia and Croatian president Franjo Tudjman. The Bosnian Serbs were also represented, but not by Karadzic; the war crimes tribunal in the Netherlands had indicted him, and he was in hiding in Bosnia. For the Americans, Secretary of State Warren Christopher oversaw the talks, with President Bill Clinton making several trips to Dayton during the three-week peace negotiations.

Slowly, the warring parties worked out a compromise. The Serbs agreed to withdraw from the Croatian territory they seized during the 1991 war. The Bosnian Serbs won the right to occupy 49 percent of Bosnia-Herzegovina; the Muslims and Croats were granted the remaining

U.S. Secretary of State Warren Christopher speaks to a peace conference organized by the United States. All of the warring parties were represented, and eventually Slobodan Milosevic agreed to give over control of Sarajevo to Bosnia-Herzegovina. The Dayton Accords were signed on November 21, 1995. Sarajevo remained in Muslim hands.

territory. As for the city of Sarajevo, Milosevic at first demanded that Bosnian Serbs be given control of the city. Izetbegovic refused. For days, the stalemate persisted and it appeared that the deadlock over Sarajevo would torpedo the peace talks.

For Milosevic, returning to Belgrade without a treaty in hand was not an option. He had already seen how the NATO forces turned the war for Sarajevo against the Bosnian Serbs. A resumption of hostilities in Bosnia would mean the continued NATO assault on the Serbian positions.

Ultimately, the Bosnian Serbs risked losing the war.

So he caved in to Izetbegovic's demands.

"You deserve Sarajevo because you've fought for it," he told Haris Silajdzic, the prime minister of Bosnia-Herzegovina. "Accordingly, since you deserve Sarajevo I am going to give it to you."

The Dayton Accords were signed on November 21, 1995.

The Bosnian Serbs seethed at the deal—they had conducted a relentless siege on Sarajevo for more than two years and came away with nothing. The city remained in Muslim hands.

Indeed, the siege took a terrible toll on the people of Sarajevo. Before the siege began, some 650,000 people lived in Sarajevo. When peace was finally declared, the population was believed to be 220,000.

During the war, hundreds of thousands of people fled the city or were killed.

As the world was shocked to learn, many of the victims were killed or imprisoned during the deadly and horrific policy that came to be known as "ethnic cleansing."

A Hurricane
of Violence

There was a dark side to the poetry of Radovan Karadzic. Even as a youth growing up in Montenegro, Karadzic used verse to predict the arrival of evil and sinister forces. At the age of 26, the young Montenegrin wrote these lines:

I hear misfortune walking
Vacant entourages passing through the city
Units of armed white poplars
Marching through the skies.

The title of that poem is "Sarajevo." Twenty years after writing those words, Karadzic would be responsible for much of the misfortune heaped on the people of Bosnia-Herzegovina.

He was born in 1944 in the waning days of World War II. Like his eventual ally Milosevic, he grew up in a Yugoslavia devastated by hunger and poverty. The Karadzic family found life particularly difficult. Radovan's father, Vuk, fought with Tito's Partisans against the Nazis, but following the war, Vuk Karadzic joined a rival faction seeking to topple

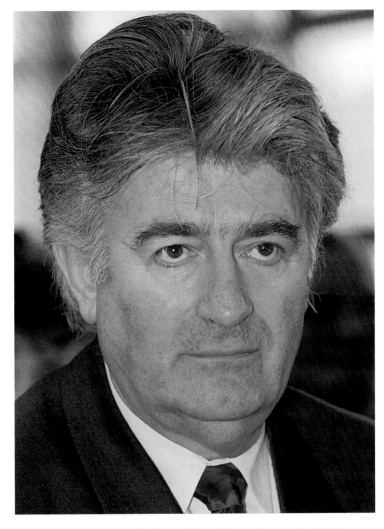

Even as a young man, Radovan Karadzic wrote poetry that fore-shadowed the dark, violent future he would bring to the people of Bosnia-Herzegovina.

the communist leader. Tito had Vuk Karadzic thrown in jail.

"I couldn't pay much attention to him as a mother," Jovanka Karadzic recalled of her son Radovan's early years. "He had his own inquisitive nature, and I had too much work. My husband was jailed for five years. Radovan was 6 months old at the time. It was a struggle. I had no wages, nothing."

Still, Karadzic was bright and studied hard. At the age of 15, the tall and husky boy was enrolled in school in Sarajevo. He eventually received a medical degree, then spent time in New York studying psychiatry. Karadzic returned to Sarajevo, married, and settled down to a career as a psychiatrist.

During his time in Sarajevo he was a rabid soccer fan, and found a job as the official team psychiatrist to the Sarajevo Red Star soccer team. Although it would seem that few amateur or professional sports teams would find a need to employ a psychiatrist, Karadzic apparently found a call for his services among the Red Star athletes. Indeed, as team psychiatrist he would often boast to his friends that his counseling of the athletes was directly responsible for their victories on the field.

"It's all related to self-glorification, all related to his own glory," said Marko Vesovic, a Sarajevo writer who knew Karadzic. "He said he could make the Red Star the best team in the world. . . . We all thought he was crazy, but he thought it was all real."

Despite the success of Red Star, Karadzic's career in Sarajevo was apparently going nowhere, because in 1983 he moved to Belgrade. He complained to friends that the ethnic Muslim majority in Sarajevo never accepted him into the city's medical community. In Belgrade he met Dobrica Cosic, a novelist and proponent of Serbian nationalism who would later serve briefly as president of the Republic of Serbia. Cosic's incandescent rhetoric calling for establishment of a south Slavic empire under the Serbs inspired many future Balkan leaders, among them Milosevic and Karadzic.

Karadzic became a committed Serb nationalist. Like Milosevic, he renounced his Montenegrin citizenship and regarded himself a Bosnian Serb. Unlike Milosevic, though, his rise to power was delayed. In 1987, Karadzic went to jail—not in the noble cause of promoting Serb nationalism, but for faking medical records for construction workers in exchange for free work and materials for a home he was building. From his jail cell, though, Karadzic became a fan of Milosevic, watching his fellow Montenegrin's rise in power. Freed from prison in 1989, Karadzic helped organize the Field of Blackbirds rally and speech in Kosovo that made Milosevic into a powerful force in Serbian politics.

In the meantime he found time to publish four volumes of poetry. For his poem "Sarajevo," Karadzic boasted of sensing dark clouds that were heading toward the city more than 20 years before the siege commenced.

"Everything I saw in terms of a fight," Karadzic said, "in terms of war, in . . . army terms. That was 20, 23 years ago, that I have written this poem, and many other poems have something of a prediction, which frightens me sometimes."

Many other poems by Karadzic are frightening. Here are a few lines from his poem "Half the Morning's Gone."

> Half the morning's gone
> Coming down the hills
> A strong and strapping wolf
> Bit half the morning off
> And in his heart it went
> Up to the hills, to the wilds.
> Every thing wept afterwards.

Sarajevo is surrounded by hills. Was the wolf coming down from the hills in reality the Bosnian Serb army? There was no question that after the Serbian attack—the bite of the wolf—there would be much weeping in Sarajevo.

Here are some lines from Karadzic's poem titled "I Surmise the Sun Is Wounding Me."

> Judges torture me for insignificant acts
> I am disgusted by the souls who radiate nothing
> Like a small nasty puppy puny death
> Is approaching from afar
> I don't know what to make of all these things
> But I can't stand the sight of you
> You file of scum
> You file of snails
> Well hurry up in your slime
> Because if I can turn my words into thunder
> I can turn you into a pool of stagnant water.

Those lines of verse show the author was showing his hatred toward somebody—perhaps the judge who sent him to jail for the medical records fraud or, perhaps, the professional medical community in Sarajevo that Karadzic believed had spurned him.

Or, perhaps, Karadzic harbored a deep hatred for the entire city of Sarajevo and its people.

■   ■   ■

While Milosevic consolidated his power in Belgrade, Karadzic returned to Sarajevo, where he organized the Serb Democratic Party. By now, he had come to Milosevic's attention; the Serbian leader regarded Karadzic as a faithful ally. In late 1991, when Milosevic ordered the creation of a secret Serbian army to lay siege to the cities of Bosnia-Herzegovina, he put Karadzic in charge. Certainly, though, Karadzic was no military leader—he was a psychiatrist. To help him direct the activities of the 90,000-man force,

General Ratko Mladic, a fierce and boastful leader, helped Radovan Karadzic direct a 90,000-man force that reigned terror over the people of Bosnia.

Karadzic enlisted the aid of General Ratko Mladic, a boastful and hard-charging commander who led a Serbian garrison in the war against the Croats.

Together, Karadzic and Mladic would oversee a reign of terror on the people of Bosnia.

Slowly, the truth started to trickle out of the Balkans. After World War II, the images of emaciated and hapless survivors of the concentration camps in Auschwitz and other places shocked the world. Leaders of civilized governments swore that type of warfare was over. But in the Balkans, it became clear that under Karadzic and Mladic, the old methods had survived.

Beatings of prisoners were reported. Muslims were said to be forced from their homes and their property stolen by invaders. Women told stories of their capture and rape by Bosnian Serb soldiers. Mass executions were said to have occurred. These types of stories first started circulating around the activities of Arkan and other paramilitary leaders, but as the war continued, it became clear that horrific "ethnic cleansing"—the forced removal and murder of all non-Serbs from Bosnia-Herzegovina—was now the policy of the Bosnian Serb leadership.

"It would be ridiculous for the commanders of this operation, Karadzic and the others, to suggest that they didn't know about any of this, or weren't in control," said British journalist Ed Vulliamy. "From what I saw with my own eyes, this was coherent, cogent, terrifying. It was a hurricane of violence and it moved with vicious and unrelenting speed across 70 percent of the country. How can you not know about that?"

By mid-1992 the Bosnia Serbs set up detention camps for Muslims they had driven out of the cities. On July 3, American newspaper reporter Roy Gutman visited one of the camps near the city of Manjaca in northern Bosnia. He wrote: "Heads bowed and hands clasped behind their backs, the Muslim prisoners lined up before their Serb captors. One by one they sat on the metal stool and then knelt to have their heads shaved. An order was given that could not be heard from 200 yards away, and each group of twenty then returned on the double to the sheds in which they lived in near darkness. Guards at the entry swung their rubber truncheons as if in anticipation of beatings to come."

Later, Gutman reported that conditions in other camps were much worse—that Muslim prisoners were being executed or starved to death. Vulliamy also found horrific conditions in a camp near the Bosnian city of Omarska. He wrote:

> The men are at various stages of human decay and affliction; the bones of their elbows and wrists protrude like pieces of jagged stone from the pencil thin stalks to which their arms have been reduced . . . There is nothing quite like the sight of the prisoner desperate to talk and to convey some terrible truth that is so near yet so far, but who dares not. Their stares burn, they speak only with their terrified silence, and eyes inflamed with the articulation of stark, undiluted, desolate fear-without-hope.

Bosnian journalist Rezak Hukanovic was imprisoned in one of the camps. He was taken into custody in the north-western Bosnian city of Prijedor. He would spend six months in the Omarska and Manjaca camps.

"Most of the time the prisoners were beaten on the way to and from the canteen where they ate," Hukanovic wrote of the Omarska camp.

> That route ran through a narrow corridor that branched off at the end and led to a staircase on the right. Upstairs, prisoners were interrogated. Back downstairs, on the left, was the canteen. The guards would pour water on a worn-out patch of

glazed cement to make the corridor more slippery. If a prisoner fell, the guards would pounce on him like famished beasts at the sight of a carcass. Using whips made of thick electrical cable, they beat the fallen prisoner all the way up the stairs for the inevitable interrogation—or simply to finish the job they had already started

For women, the tortures they endured under the Bosnian Serbs also included rape. American journalist Peter Maass wrote of the systematic rapes of female Muslim detainees at the Trnopolje camp, as described by one high-school-age prisoner:

> Three days after her arrival at the prison, she went with a large number of women and other girls to fetch water from a well about 50 meters from the prison gates. Returning from the well, Trnopolje guards held back six girls . . . and stopped them from re-entering the prison gates. They were then joined by four more female prisoners. The guards took the 10 girls to a house across the meadow. They were taken to the side yard of the house, out of sight of the roadway. Thirty Serbian soldiers—including "some dressed like a tank crew"—were there and they taunted the girls, calling them "Turkish whores."

The prisoners were then raped.

As these stories found their way into the international press, Karadzic and the other Bosnian leaders first denied them, claiming they were lies planted by the Muslims to sway public opinion to their side. Soon, though, it became impossible to deny the truth. And even then, Karadzic insisted, the atrocities were being committed by terrorists and not members of the Bosnian Serb army.

"Muslim civilians are free to stay or to leave," he said in a radio broadcast. "The terrorist elements may cause further troubles, but people, civilians . . . are completely safe and secure. Simply, our army is very, very responsible."

And then came Srebrenica, and now the stories could no longer be denied.

The town is located on the Drina River, and included a large population of Muslims. The city stood directly in the path of Karadzic's plan to establish a separate Bosnian Serb republic along the Drina. For two years, the Serbs had surrounded the town; like the Sarajevans, the citizens of Srebrenica managed to hold off the aggressors. But finally, on July 12, 1995, the Muslim defenses fell and Mladic's troops marched into Srebrenica. The attack was relentless. More than 6,000 Muslims, mostly men and boys, were massacred by Mladic's men in the two-day attack on the town.

Karadzic stood by the actions of Mladic's men, claiming the Bosnian Serbs fired on the Muslims in self-defense. He also denied the death toll was as high as the press reported.

"Can you imagine how many of our own people would have been killed if Mladic had not taken this measure?" Karadzic told reporters. "It was a desperate measure on our side confronted with an overwhelmingly powerful enemy. We were in an absolutely desperate situation."

Government leaders in the West recognized Karadzic's denials as hollow half-truths. In America, Vice President Al Gore recalled the shock of learning of the Srebrenica massacre. Gore said his daughter had seen news coverage of the massacre, and was horrified at a photograph of a Muslim woman who hanged herself from a tree rather than surrender to the Bosnian Serbs.

"My 21-year-old daughter asked me about that picture,"

An investigator sifts through the rubble at a mass grave near Srebencia, the site of one of the worst massacres in the entire conflict. Though Radovan Karadzic claimed they fired in self-defense, Bosnian Serbs, under the command of Ratko Mladic, brutally slaughtered more than 6,000 Muslims.

Gore said. "What am I supposed to tell her? Why is this happening and we're not doing anything? . . . My daughter is surprised the world is allowing this to happen. I am too."

Mladic did not intend to stop in Srebrenica. Next, his

troops overran the town of Zepa and were prepared to launch an assault on a third city, Gorazde, when NATO announced it would launch air strikes unless Mladic's men were reined in. Soon, under the terms of the Dayton Accords, NATO ground troops would be assigned to peacekeeping duties in Bosnia-Herzegovina.

Meanwhile, in the Netherlands, the United Nations established the International Criminal Tribunal for the Former Yugoslavia to investigate the stories of atrocities coming out of the Balkans.

"I'm absolutely determined that we must concentrate our efforts in investigating cases that hold the promise of taking us as high up the chain of command as the evidence will reveal," announced Louise Arbour, a Canadian judge appointed to head the tribunal.

By 1995 Karadzic and Mladic were under indictment for war crimes. The indictments charged them with "genocide as well as numerous crimes against humanity, including hostage-taking of peacekeepers, destruction of sacred places, torture of captured civilians and wanton destruction of private property." In late 1995, when the leaders of the Balkan states were invited to Dayton to negotiate a peace treaty, Karadzic, the leader of the Bosnian Serbs, could not go. By setting foot in America he would assuredly have been arrested.

Some war criminals were brought to justice. Among the first to be arrested was Dusan Tadic, who helped run the Omarska detention camp. He was charged with ordering the murders and rapes of Muslim prisoners. Tadic was convicted after a trial at The Hague and sentenced to a lengthy prison term. Other Bosnian Serb leaders faced charges as well. In Hukanovic's hometown of Prijedor, the chief of police, Simo Drljaca, was shot dead trying to escape from United Nations troops, who had a warrant for his arrest.

Though he was later convicted of ordering the rape and murder of Muslim prisoners, Dusan Tardic ran the Omarska detention camp with an iron fist for over four years. He was among the first war criminals brought to justice, but these prisoners felt the brunt of his brutality.

As for Mladic and Karadzic, even after their indictments and the NATO intervention in Bosnia, the two men remained at large. Karadzic surrounded himself with armed protectors and, for a time, lived openly in the Bosnian city of Pale, boasting that he was beyond the reach of authorities. Milosevic refused to turn over the two criminals, claiming he had no control over them.

While living in Pale, Karadzic appeared often on television and gave press interviews, encouraging Bosnian Serbs to rise up against the NATO peacekeepers.

But Western diplomats kept up their pressure on Milosevic. Finally, in July 1996, the Yugoslavian president convinced Karadzic to resign as head of the Serb Democratic Party as well as the presidency of the phony Bosnian Serb Republic.

Still, Karadzic and Mladic evaded capture, fleeing under the protection of Bosnian Serbs. Even Karadzic's mother has said she doesn't know where he is. "It's very hard when people start saying he is here and there," said Jovanka Karadzic. "They said he was in the mountains. They wrote in the papers that he was in Russia, after that, that he was somewhere else. All those things are being said."

The U.S. State Department has offered a reward of $5 million for information leading to the arrests of Karadzic and Mladic.

The two war criminals remain at large.

6

Only Freedom

Just past noon on the last Saturday in February 1998, a Serbian police car on routine patrol outside Drenica, Kosovo, was ambushed by a group of Muslim guerrilla fighters. The Serbian driver lost control of the car and flipped over into a ditch. Another Serbian police car sped to the assistance of the crashed vehicle. When that patrol car arrived, a gun fight ensued between the policemen and the guerrillas. During the gun battle, two of the Serbian policemen were killed, while the other two were seriously wounded.

Soon, the region of central Kosovo would be swarming with Serbian police. The policemen flooded into the village of Drenica, where they burned and looted homes and killed 53 Kosovars they believed to be members of the militant Kosovo Liberation Army (KLA). The ambush of the police car followed by the typically bloody Serbian retaliation sparked what would become the fourth war to sweep through the former Yugoslavia in seven years. Despite heading a government staggered by the costs of the wars in Slovenia, Croatia, and Bosnia-Herzegovina,

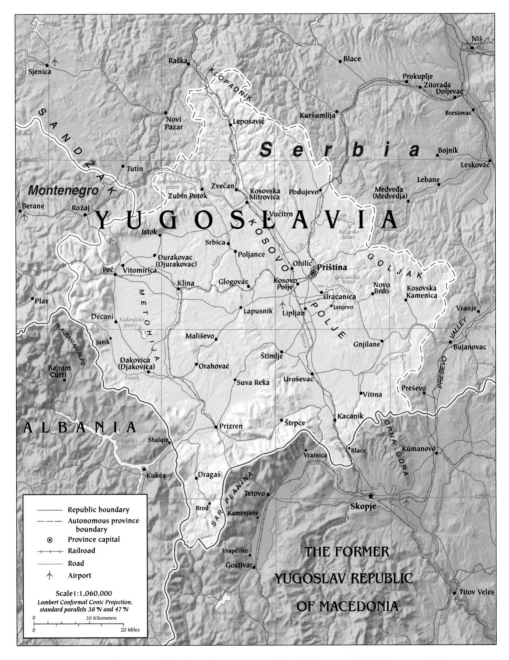

A map of Kosovo, the site of great turmoil and dispute, which does not fully show the dry, rock nature of the land. Kosovo would eventually become a central point in the Balkans conflict.

Slobodan Milosevic did not hesitate to commit his army to wiping out a group of militant ethnic Albanians in Kosovo fighting to establish an independent nation.

"Many innocent people were killed in that attack, including women and children," said Fred Abrahams, a representative of the New York–based Human Rights Watch. "In villages nearby, there were cases where the evidence strongly suggests summary executions. That is, Albanians were killed by the police after having been taken into detention."

And so, it seemed as though the tactics of war in the Balkans hadn't changed, even though NATO troops were acting as peacekeepers in Bosnia-Herzegovina and the United Nations war crimes tribunal was keeping a close watch on events in Kosovo, where trouble had been brewing for years.

Indeed, friction between the Serbs and Muslims dated back to the Turkish conquest of the Balkan states. Following the First Balkan War, the Treaty of London established an independent Albanian nation just south of Serbia. About half the ethnic Albanians living in the region found themselves citizens of the new country; the other half remained behind in what would become the province of Kosovo.

Kosovo was also populated by a Serbian minority; the two ethnic groups became uneasy neighbors. The Serbs considered Kosovo hallowed ground—it was, after all, the location of the Field of Blackbirds.

During World War II the Italians invaded Albania, annexed Kosovo, and set up a puppet government. When Kosovo returned to Yugoslavia following World War II, Tito considered the province a part of Serbia, but he permitted the Kosovars a large degree of autonomy: they were allowed their own provincial parliament in the

Kosovo capital of Pristina, although, of course, they would come under the ultimate authority of the communist government in Belgrade. By the late 1980s, 2.1 million people lived in Kosovo, more than half of them ethnic Albanians.

Even under Tito the Kosovars were forced to endure terrible poverty. Unlike the fertile lands elsewhere in Yugoslavia, the Kosovo terrain was dry, rocky, and not tillable for farming. Many Kosovars had to rely on relatives in Albania and other Muslim states to send them money and food. The Muslims in Kosovo also found themselves alienated from the public school system established by the communist government in Belgrade; as devout Muslims, they insisted on starting their own ethnic Albanian schools.

In 1989, when Slobodan Milosevic came to power in Yugoslavia, he suppressed many of the Kosovars' rights, including closing the Albanian schools. Police were given authority to rough up Kosovars, harass them on their streets, and steal from their shops. Kosovars quietly, and with dignity, endured the abuses.

Once Yugoslavia disintegrated with Slovenia, Macedonia, Croatia, and Bosnia-Herzegovina declaring their independence, ethnic Albanians in Kosovo started agitating for independence as well. For much of the 1990s, they were largely held in check by Ibrahim Rugova, who in 1989 founded the Democratic League of Kosovo, the largest political party in the province. In 1991, Rugova would be elected president of the Republic of Kosovo, an independent nation recognized by no one except the Kosovars.

Rugova was an admirer of the Indian leader Mahatma Gandhi and the American civil rights leader Martin Luther King Jr. Both men preached nonviolent resistance, and Rugova counseled the militant members of his

Ibrahim Rugova, elected president of the Republic of Kosovo in 1991, followed the teachings of Mahatma Ghandi and Martin Luther King Jr. He managed to keep the peace for many years until the more militant members of his movement eventually broke free and used violence to make their statements.

movement to follow the examples set by King and Gandhi. For seven years, they remained patient, but by the late 1990s calls for armed resistance against Serbs were starting to surface among the militants.

By 1996, with NATO troops keeping the peace in Bosnia-Herzegovina, the militant agitators in Kosovo believed the time had come to strike. Guns and arms were smuggled into Kosovo from sympathizers in Albania. As for the government in Albania, President Sali Berisha—a native Kosovar himself—made no secret of his desire for the province to secede from Yugoslavia.

"It is very clear for the Kosovo people that their freedom and rights will not come as a gift from anyone and their problems will not be solved in . . . Belgrade, or Washington, London and Paris," he said. "They are solved and will be solved in Pristina and the towns and villages of Kosovo."

As for Milosevic, he preached the same fierce nationalistic rhetoric that had led Serbs into wars in Slovenia, Croatia, and Bosnia-Herzegovina. He insisted that Kosovo was sacred ground to the Serbs and, in fact, home to nearly a million of his countrymen. He would never let Kosovo go.

On the evening of April 22, 1996, three Serbs sat down for drinks at a cafe in Decani in western Kosovo. Just before 8:30 P.M., three men wearing masks walked into the cafe and opened fire with automatic weapons. The three Serbs who died in the attack were the first victims of the Kosovo Liberation Army.

Asked by a reporter what the Kosovo Liberation Army sought to achieve, KLA supporter Florim Krasniqi said, "Simple. Freedom. Freedom and freedom. Only freedom."

With so much blood already spilled in the Balkans, Western diplomats saw a conflict in Kosovo on the horizon and did what they could to keep tempers from boiling over. But Lord David Owen, a British diplomat, found himself frustrated by the unwillingness of the Kosovo Liberation Army to back down. "These are not people you can do business with," he said.

The KLA struck several more times over the next two years. It appeared their aim was not to defeat the Yugoslavian army but to provoke the Serbs into a fight and then seek protection from NATO, hopefully obtaining a treaty brokered by western diplomats that would guarantee them independence. Finally, they hoped to share in some $5 billion in foreign aid that was pouring into Slovenia, Croatia, and Bosnia-Herzegovina to help those war-torn republics rebuild.

And so, for the next two years the KLA staged a series of guerrilla attacks on Serbs in Kosovo. Elsewhere, student militants in Kosovo agitated for independence. Yugoslavian authorities always struck back at the attacks and demonstrations—usually with their typical brutishness.

Following the attack on the road to Drenica, the Serbs ratcheted the stakes up a notch. Police swept into Drenica aboard armored vehicles and in helicopters, strafing the town with gunfire. To the hapless residents of Drenica, it was clear that the policy of ethnic cleansing had not been buried with the Dayton Accords. Passions were further inflamed when a news crew filmed bulldozers burying the mutilated bodies of the dead Kosovars into a mass grave, enraging Muslims because the burial violated the strict rituals for the dead specified in Islamic law. Western diplomats were horrified by the pictures as well. They urged Milosevic to meet with the Kosovars and address their demands. He refused.

Kosovo teetered on the edge of all-out war. More guerrilla attacks by the KLA were staged. Police responded by skirmishing with the militants. Finally, in May, Milosevic and Rugova met briefly in Belgrade; their meeting accomplished nothing.

In June, Milosevic ordered a full military offensive against the KLA. Until then, KLA troops controlled about

A Kosovo Liberation Army soldier stands guard while one of his fellow KLA soldiers is buried. The KLA fought successfully against the Serbs in minor skirmishes until Milosevic ordered a full military offensive against the KLA and innocent Kosovars, 200,00 of which were forced over the border into Albania.

40 percent of the country, but faced with the overwhelming force of the Yugoslavian army, the guerrilla fighters were unable to hold their ground. Milosevic ordered a relentless attack not only on the KLA but also on innocent Kosovars. He had them driven from their homes. He had

their villages burned and their shops looted and bulldozed. He had Albanian men arrested and executed. Some 200,000 Kosovars were driven into the countryside, forced to live without shelter.

"They're somewhere in the woods hiding, the women, the children, the elderly," said Josef Hajrizi, editor of *Illyria,* an Albanian-American newspaper. "My brothers, I have two brothers there—they have guns, they've armed themselves and they're trying to defend [their] village. And last week I spoke to them and they said . . . until the last man goes down, this village is not going to fall."

The fighting lasted all summer. Not only were the Kosovars hunted by the Yugoslavian army, but now vicious paramilitary units such as Arkan's Tigers had also entered the fray. The Tigers used the same brutish tactics on the Kosovars they had inflicted on the Bosnians and Croats.

Here is how *Koha Ditore,* an Albanian newspaper, reported the murders of 11 members of the Ahmeti family in the Likoshan region of Kosovo: "Five or six big bloodstains, broken teeth, brains all over the place, a piece of human jaw hanging down from the bushes, bullets of different calibers, are seen at the scene of the crime."

Western diplomats were alarmed at the return of ethnic cleansing. But the success of the Yugoslavian attacks worried western diplomats for another reason: would Milosevic, emboldened by his success against the Kosovars, pursue the KLA over the border and into Albania? By attacking Albania, Milosevic would turn a civil war into a war between two nations. By now, Albania had its own problems. The government of President Sali Berisha had fallen; the nation was in turmoil as rival groups wrestled for power. Clearly, diplomats knew it would be an easy matter for Milosevic's troops to take advantage of the chaos and continue their ethnic cleansing across the border.

In September, evidence of another massacre in Kosovo turned up in the village of Gornje Obrinje—the bodies of 16 people were found, murdered by gunshots fired at close range. Ten of the victims were women, children, and elderly people.

The massacre at Gornje Obrinje prompted President Bill Clinton to dispatch former U.S. senator Bob Dole on a diplomatic mission to Kosovo and then to Belgrade, where he warned Milosevic to cease hostilities or NATO would start bombing.

At first, Milosevic appeared to back down. He agreed to withdraw his troops but seethed at the heavy hand shown by the Americans and other NATO leaders. Instead of withdrawing the troops, he ordered reinforcements and supplies sent deeper into Kosovo. As for the bulk of the Yugoslavian army, he directed his commanders to ring the province with troops. Thousands of Serbs took positions along the Kosovo border in what Milosevic called "Operation Horseshoe."

The secret military buildup hardly remained secret for long. NATO was not fooled—the alliance employs the world's most sophisticated satellite surveillance equipment designed specifically to follow enemy troop movements. What's more, the Yugoslavian troops supposedly hiding along the border couldn't keep their guns in their holsters. By early December, they were skirmishing with Kosovo guerrillas. On December 14, more than 30 guerrillas were killed in a five-hour battle with Yugoslavian troops near the Kosovo village of Malisevo.

Milosevic ordered another offensive. On January 18, 1999, the bodies of 45 murdered civilians were discovered in the village of Racak. This crime carried the thumbprint of the paramilitary fighters—witnesses said a small group of hooded men dressed in black carried out the murders.

Milosevic exhibited little feeling for the Racak victims. He insisted they were killed by other Kosovars to draw sympathy. "This is not a massacre," he boasted. "It was staged. These people were terrorists."

The United States decided it was time to bomb Yugoslavia, but other NATO members asked for one more attempt to negotiate a peaceful settlement. On February 6, diplomats from the NATO alliance met with Yugoslavian and KLA leaders in a hunting lodge at Rambouillet, near Paris. Little was accomplished. KLA leader Adem Demaqi demanded independence for Kosovo within three years, along with a NATO peacekeeping force to keep an eye on the Serbs. The Yugoslavian negotiators—Milosevic refused to attend—told the diplomats they were prepared to grant Kosovo some measure of autonomy, but they refused to permit Western troops on Kosovo soil. The peace conference broke up with no accord in hand.

On March 18, NATO issued one last warning to Milosevic: further atrocities committed in Kosovo would unleash an air strike on Yugoslavia. In response, Milosevic moved more troops to the Kosovo border.

Just five years before, Milosevic witnessed how the awesome power of NATO swung the battle for Sarajevo against the Bosnian Serbs. Not a single NATO plane was shot down by the Bosnian Serb ground defenses. NATO cruise missiles wiped out the Bosnian Serb military command at Banja Luka in one devastating blow. Could Milosevic actually believe the army he had at his command posed any threat to the most powerful military alliance in history?

Diplomats and military aides who knew Milosevic later said the Yugoslavian president never believed NATO would carry out its threat to bomb his country. When his top military adviser, General Momcilo Perisic, told him

An Albanian witnesses a mass grave at Racak, the site of one of the worst offensives in the Balkan conflict. It carried the signature of the most brutal Serbian paramilitary fighters and brought the intense scrutiny of NATO on Milosevic.

the NATO leaders weren't bluffing, Milosevic fired him. When American diplomat Christopher Hill delivered one of the final ultimatums to Milosevic, the Yugoslavian leader responded, "You are a superpower. You can do what you want."

On March 20, Milosevic sent his troops back into Kosovo. Thousands of Kosovars were driven from their homes, many were murdered by Yugoslavian army units. Entire villages were burned to the ground by the invading army.

Four days later, NATO hit Yugoslavia.

Ironically, in Belgrade, a movie retelling the saga of Lazar Hrebeljanovic on the Field of Blackbirds played on television when the bombs started falling on the city. In Kosovo, the Yugoslavian army stepped up its attack. The Kosovo town of Stimlje was leveled by Yugoslavian troops on the first night of the bombing. "The earth was burning, from the ground and from the sky, and it seemed there was nowhere to hide," said Fehmi Baftiu, an Indian human rights worker stationed in Kosovo.

There was no question, though, that the NATO bombing had the desired impact on the hearts and minds of the Serbs. Throughout the conflicts in Slovenia, Croatia, and Bosnia-Herzegovina, the Serbs had been sheltered from the fighting—none of those countries had armies capable of posing a threat to the powerful Serbs. But now, their homes were shaking as NATO bombs fell throughout Yugoslavia.

Milosevic made half-hearted gestures to end the fighting. He offered a partial withdrawal of troops from Kosovo, but NATO refused his terms and the bombing continued. By early May, Serbs started demonstrating in the streets for an end to the bombing. The three previous wars had bankrupted the Serbian people; now, the NATO bombing had knocked out their water and electric plants. Life in Belgrade was starting to resemble what life in Sarajevo had been like five years earlier—full of hardship, danger, and hunger.

On May 12, NATO announced it would expand its strikes against nonmilitary targets. One of those targets was the residence of Slobodan Milosevic; it was destroyed by a NATO bomb. The president was not home when his house was leveled. Other targets included the headquarters for

Milosevic's political party, Belgrade radio and television stations, and several government buildings. Airports, military bases, bridges, utilities, railroad lines, chemical plants, and other factories were all destroyed.

NATO did suffer some setbacks during the bombing. On March 27, an American F-117A stealth fighter—one of the most sophisticated weapons in the NATO arsenal—was shot down by the Yugoslavian ground defenses. The pilot was rescued in a dramatic mission staged by American commandos, but the Serbs had the burnt remains of the plane to show off to reporters, giving them one brief opportunity during the war to boast about the courage of their defenders.

Despite that one tiny victory, though, it was clear the Yugoslavian cities were suffering from the constant pounding.

And as devastating as the bombing had been on the Serbs, the Yugoslavian army offensive over the past year had all but wiped out Muslim civilization in Kosovo. It is believed that during the fighting some 800,000 ethnic Albanians lost their lives or were driven out of their homes by the invaders.

In late May, NATO leaders announced they were prepared to carry out the next phase in the assault—an invasion of Serbia by ground troops. On May 26, NATO planes carried out one of the most intense nights of bombing since the siege began. The next day, the war crimes tribunal in The Hague announced it had indicted Milosevic for authorizing the ethnic cleansing of Kosovo.

Milosevic realized that continuing the war would be both foolish and futile.

On June 2, Yugoslavia surrendered.

Milosevic agreed to a peace agreement drafted by former Russian premier Viktor S. Chernomyrdin, who had been

The town of Pristina was heavily damaged during the NATO bombing raids. This devastated police barracks shows just how thorough the attacks were and why, eventually, it led to Milosevic's realization that surrender of Yugoslavia was finally necessary.

appointed by his government as a special envoy to the Balkan states. The agreement specified that Yugoslavia would continue to exercise a largely symbolic sovereignty over Kosovo, and that a United Nations peacekeeping force would remain in Kosovo. The Serbs agreed to withdraw from Kosovo on June 6.

On the night of June 10, Slobodan Milosevic appeared on television to address his people. Even in the face of a humiliating loss, the president appealed to the Serbs' fierce ethnic pride, hoping his people would look upon their defeat as they regarded the defeat by Lazar Hrebeljanovic 700 years before on the Field of Blackbirds—a moment of great national dignity.

"This is another great achievement of our defense," he told the Serbs. "The entire people participated in this

war, from babies in hospitals to intensive care patients to soldiers in air-defense positions and soldiers on the border. The people are the heroes of this war."

This time, the Serbs would not be fooled.

Sitting in their unheated homes in their devastated cities, lacking clean water and electricity, and with no money to buy food, clothes, and the other necessities of life, the people of Yugoslavia had by now decided there were no heroes in Slobodan Milosevic's wars.

7

Arrest

Nicolae Ceausescu ruled Romania with an iron fist for 22 years. With the backing of the powerful Soviet government, the communist dictator threw his enemies in prison, stifled personal freedoms, and kept his people impoverished while he amassed an enormous personal wealth. But as communism collapsed in the Soviet Union, Ceausescu lost the protection he enjoyed from his once-powerful allies. In Romania, the people rose up against the dictator. On Christmas Day in 1989, Ceausescu was executed by a firing squad.

A similar fate awaited Erich Honecker, the dictator who came to power in communist East Germany in 1971. Under Honecker's rule, East Germany became one of the most oppressive regimes in Europe. Honecker maintained a secret police force to spy on East Germans. At the Berlin Wall, which separated East Berlin from West Berlin, Honecker ordered guards to shoot Berliners attempting to escape to the free sector of the city. When the Soviets could no longer protect Honecker, his power evaporated. Honecker was arrested and jailed briefly, then kicked out of the country. He died in exile in Chile.

In Yugoslavia, Slobodan Milosevic watched the walls closing in on him and feared his regime would end in humiliation, trial, and execution.

He led Yugoslavians into four wars in less than 10 years and won no lasting victories. He was responsible for some of the worst suffering by civilians in the post-World War II years. He had been indicted for war crimes by the Hague tribunal. His capital city of Belgrade was devastated by bombing. By the fall of 2000, Serbs had taken to the streets demanding the ouster of Milosevic. On October 5, the country

After years of violence, terror and unspeakable atrocities, Slobodan Milosevic finally sits before a war crimes tribunal in The Hague.

staged elections. Emerging as victors were two new leaders —Vojislav Kostunica and Zoran Djindjic.

The two men were hardly allies. Kostunica was cut from the mold of Milosevic—a strongly nationalistic Serb who harbored a deep ethnic pride. He hated the NATO nations for bringing destruction to his country. He was able to win the presidency by appealing to hard-line Serbs as well as others who believed he could rebuild the republic.

Meanwhile, unrest was occurring elsewhere in Yugoslavia.

In the early 1990s, when the other republics voted to secede, Montenegro remained a loyal republic. But over the years Montenegrins slowly developed a hostility toward the aggressive Serbs; finally, in April 2001, voters in Montenegro adopted a referendum calling for independence. Such independent thinking may have provoked attacks and ethnic cleansing during Milosevic's rule; now, Kostunica could do little but let events in Montenegro take their course.

As for Milosevic, Kostunica realized the former dictator was still popular among many hard-line and ethnically proud Serbs.

Djindjic, on the other hand, looked on the Western democracies as potential allies and the source of aid he knew Yugoslavia would need to rebuild following the NATO bombings. He was elected prime minister, the second highest government post in the nation. He became a strong voice in Yugoslavia for bringing Milosevic to justice. Djindjic harbored presidential ambitions himself and believed Milosevic's arrest would ultimately prove to be popular among the Serbian people.

But it would not be easy. Although he left the presidency in October 2000, Milosevic refused to leave the presidential palace—a mansion in Belgrade known as the Oval House that Tito had occupied. Even out of office, Milosevic still counted many Serbs as his allies who aimed to protect the former dictator rather than see him stand trial for war crimes. The appearance of Slobodan Milosevic standing in shackles before a tribunal in The Hague was not a spectacle many Serbs wanted to see—they were sure that Milosevic's trial would feature terrible evidence of atrocities that would implicate not only the former Yugoslavian leader but many other officials in the government—some of whom still held power.

As for Milosevic, he ignored calls from prosecutors in The Hague demanding his arrest. Living in the Oval

House, he gave out newspaper interviews and encouraged his supporters to denounce the Hague indictment.

"I always considered myself to be an ordinary person, whom, at one point in life, historical circumstances placed in a position to devote his whole life to the nation that had everything in jeopardy," he told a reporter shortly after he left office.

Those words hardly sounded like they were spoken by somebody willing to take responsibility for ethnic cleansing or the murders and displacement of some 400,000 Sarajevans and 800,000 Kosovars. In Yugoslavia as well as the Western states, officials started calling for the arrest of Milosevic.

The United States turned up the most pressure. In Washington, Congress agreed to make $40 million available to the Yugoslavian government to help rebuild the nation following the NATO attacks. But the State Department—which carries out America's diplomatic policies—refused to release the money until Milosevic was brought to justice.

In Belgrade, Western diplomats found Djindjic willing to turn Milosevic over to the Hague tribunal. But Kostunica resisted.

Djindjic decided to make his move without the president's approval. On March 30, 2001, Kostunica was out of the country, attending a conference in Geneva, Switzerland. As prime minister, Djindjic controlled the Serbian police, but not the army. That night, he ordered the police to arrest Milosevic. When the police arrived at the presidential mansion they found the property surrounded by soldiers, who were under orders not to let the police pass. After a brief standoff, the police officers retreated.

Kostunica hurried back to Belgrade, where he was met by a furious Djindjic. The two leaders met for three hours. Finally, Djindjic was able to convince Kostunica to turn

Serbian Prime Minister, Zoran Djindjic, ordered the police under his command to arrest Milosevic. They were met with resistance by the Serbian army and former members of the paramilitary groups.

Milosevic over to the war crimes tribunal.

Emerging from the meeting, a weary Kostunica told reporters, "If you start something, you have to finish it."

Kostunica ordered the army to retreat from its positions around the Oval House. They were quickly replaced by about 100 armed men, former members of the vicious paramilitary groups. They were led by Sinisa Vucinic, who had led a paramilitary force in Bosnia-Herzegovina known as the Falcons.

At 2 A.M. on March 31, 120 Belgrade policemen donned dark civilian clothes and pulled black ski masks over their heads. They arrived at the Oval House minutes later and took up positions surrounding the property. Next, 20 armed police officers scaled iron gates at the front of the property. They were met by gunfire from Vucinic's paramilitary fighters. The policemen quickly retreated, and for the next several minutes the two sides traded gunfire.

The police and paramilitary fighters found themselves at a standoff. Dawn broke over Belgrade with no resolution to the crisis. Outside the palace, a crowd of thousands of people had gathered to watch the drama unfold. Many of them built bonfires in the Belgrade streets and raised banners demanding Milosevic's surrender; others considered the former president a national hero. There were many clashes in the crowd as tempers flared.

Inside the Oval House, Milosevic remained under the protection of his paramilitary supporters. Meanwhile, the police cut the electricity and water to the mansion.

Night fell again over Belgrade. Inside the Oval House, Milosevic knew the standoff could not last forever. It became clear to the former dictator that he would have to submit to arrest or face death from a policeman's bullet when Kostunica and Djindjic finally gave the order to storm the residence. During the standoff, friends said that Milosevic brandished a gun and threatened to kill himself.

Just before 2 A.M. on April 1—nearly a day after the standoff began—Yugoslavian government officials delivered a written promise to Milosevic that he would be given a fair trial on state charges that had been prepared against him. In Yugoslavia, the former president had been charged with diverting state funds to his own use and mismanaging the Yugoslavian economy. Milosevic was told that he would not be facing the more serious Hague charges immediately, although he was told that extradition to the Netherlands was likely.

Milosevic read the letter slowly and carefully, his mind and body weary from the ordeal. Finally, he gave them his response. Gone were his fiery words that preached Serbian nationalism and ethnic pride, gone was the angry rhetoric that inspired his followers to rape and murder.

"This is very funny," Milosevic said with a wry smile, then told the government negotiators he was prepared to surrender.

At 4:45 A.M., Slobodan Milosevic was placed in handcuffs and marched out of the Oval House in Belgrade, taking the

After a decade of brutality, Yugoslav Special Forces enter the house of Slobodan Milosevic and eventually took him into custody. As Milosevic was driven away in the back of a police car, his daughter, Marija, ran out of the house and fired five shots into the air with a pistol.

first steps toward his trial on crimes against humanity.

He was placed in the back seat of a police car. As the car started driving slowly off the grounds of the presidential palace, Milosevic's 35-year-old daughter Marija suddenly emerged from the house.

Marija Milosevic ran into the courtyard. In her hand she held her father's gun. Suddenly, the woman held the gun aloft and fired off five bursts, startling the crowd that had gathered outside the gates.

The bullets soared into the night sky, the last desperate but futile shots fired in the 1,000-year struggle by the Serbs to rule a south Slavic empire.

Alas, they fell harmlessly to the ground.

5TH CENTURY To escape German invaders, Slavic people in Poland make their way south to the mountainous Balkan region along the Adriatic Sea.

1172 Serb Stefan Dusan forges the first south Slavic empire.

1389 Lazar Hrebeljanovic defeated by the Ottoman Turks on the Field of Blackbirds in Kosovo; the battle would inspire future Serb nationalism.

1815 Armies under the Karadjordjevic and Obrenovic families drive the Turks out of Serbia; the two families share power in Serbia into the 20th century.

1878 Congress of Berlin awards territory in Bosnia-Herzegovina to Austria-Hungary; the treaty enrages Serbs and is regarded as a contributing factor to World War I.

1912 First Balkan War pits Serbia and Montenegro against Turkey.

1913 In the Second Balkan War, Serbs and Greeks defeat Bulgarians and Turks.

1914 Serb Gavrilo Princip assassinates Archduke Franz Ferdinand, touching off World War I.

1918 At the end of World War I, the Corfu Declaration creates the Kingdom of the Serbs, Croats, and Slovenes.

1928 King Alexander Karadjordjevic abolishes provincial borders and renames the country Yugoslavia.

1939 Start of World War II; Yugoslavia partitioned by the Germans and ruled by Croatian fascists.

1941 Slobodan Milosevic born in Pozarevac, Serbia.

1944 Radovan Karadzic born in Montenegro.

1945 Croatian communist Josep Broz, known as Tito, emerges as Yugoslavian head of state.

1948 Tito breaks away from Soviet influence, establishing an independent communist state and a policy of neutrality. At home, he forces the country's hostile ethnic groups to live in a united society.

1980 Tito dies, turning over presidency to a yearly rotation of rulers.

1984 Sarajevo hosts the 1984 Winter Olympics.

1986 Milosevic selected to head Communist Party in Serbia.

1989 In a speech on the Field of Blackbirds, Milosevic promises Serbs they will head a south Slav empire; later, Milosevic named president of Yugoslavia.

1990 Communist Party of Yugoslavia disintegrates over calls for secession by Croatia and Slovenia.

1991 In June, Croatia and Slovenia declare independence from the former Yugoslavia; Yugoslavian soldiers and paramilitary fighters invade both republics in separate military actions. In November, Karadzic organizes a Bosnian Serb army. Also, Kosovars vote to establish Republic of Kosovo.

1992 Bosnia-Herzegovina declares its independence; Bosnian Serbs take arms and, aided by paramilitary fighters, the siege of Sarajevo and war elsewhere in the country begin. Western journalists report atrocities committed under the policy of "ethnic cleansing."

1994 Mortar fire kills 69 people waiting for bread in Sarajevo; the attack prompts NATO commanders to order air strikes on Bosnian Serb positions.

1995 Six thousand Muslims massacred by Bosnian Serbs at Srebrenica; Dayton Accords end the war. Karadzic and Bosnian Serb General Ratko Mladic indicted for war crimes.

1996 Kosovo Liberation Army murders three Serb civilians at a café in Decani, Kosovo.

1997 Paramilitary leader Zeljko Raznatovic, known as Arkan, indicted for war crimes.

1998 Serb military massacres 53 ethnic Albanians in the village of Drenica, Kosovo, touching off the fourth Balkan war since 1991.

1999 NATO bombs Belgrade to halt Serb attacks on Kosovo.

2000 Arkan assassinated in Belgrade; Milosevic driven from the Yugoslavian presidency.

2001 Montenegro votes for independence; Milosevic arrested for war crimes.

BOOKS AND PERIODICALS:

Anderson, Raymond H. "Giant Among Communists Governed Like a Monarch." *The New York Times,* 5 May 1980.

Binder, David. "Tito: The Fighter-Survivor Who Unified a Country." *The New York Times,* 5 May 1980.

Calabresi, Massimo. "My Tea with Arkan the Henchman." *Time,* 12 April 1999.

Dizdarevic, Zlatko. *Sarajevo: A War Journal.* New York: Fromm International, 1993.

Portraits of Sarajevo. New York: Fromm International, 1994.

Doder, Dusko, and Louise Branson. *Milosevic: Portrait of a Tyrant.* New York: The Free Press, 1999.

Erlanger, Steven. "For Serbs in Croatia, a Pledge Unkept." *The New York Times,* 16 January 2000.

"Suspect in Serbian War Crimes Murdered by Masked Gunmen." *The New York Times,* 16 January 2000.

"Political Motive Suspected in Killing of Serbian Warlord." *The New York Times,* 17 January 2000.

"Milosevic Government Denies Role in Killing of Serbian Warlord." *The New York Times,* 19 January 2000.

"After the Arrest: Wider Debate About the Role of Milosevic, and of Serbia." *The New York Times,* 2 April 2001.

"Yugoslav Chief Says Milosevic Shouldn't Be Sent to Hague." *The New York Times,* 3 April 2001.

"Admissions by Milosevic Should Speed His Trial, Bosnia Says." *The New York Times,* 4 April 2001.

"The Balkan Disease Isn't Cured Yet." *The New York Times,* 15 April 2001.

Erlanger, Steven, and Carlotta Gall. "Milosevic Arrest Came with Pledge for a Fair Trial." *The New York Times,* 2 April 2001.

"Foe of the Warlord Arkan Slain in Belgrade." Agence France-Presse, 21 March 2000.

Gall, Carlotta. "Witness Ties Ex-Police Boss to Killing of Warlord." *The New York Times,* 8 March 2001.

"Milosevic Faces New Charges for Standoff at His Compound." *The New York Times,* 3 April 2001.

"Geography and Ethnic Diversity Shape Yugoslavia." *The New York Times,* 5 May 1980.

Glenny, Misha. *The Balkans.* New York: Penguin Books, 1999.

Holbrooke, Richard. *To End a War.* New York: Random House, 1998.

Hukanovic, Rezak. *The Tenth Circle of Hell: A Memoir of Life in the Death Camps of Bosnia.* New York: Basic Books, 1996.

Kifner, John. "An Outlaw in the Balkans Is Basking in the Spotlight." *The New York Times,* 23 November 1993.

Maass, Peter. *Love Thy Neighbor: A Story of War.* New York: Alfred A. Knopf, 1996.

McGeary, Johanna. "The Road to Hell." *Time,* 12 April 1999.

Middleton, Drew. "Belgrade's Defense Strategy: Guerrilla War." *The New York Times,* 5 May 1980.

Morrow, Lance. "The Balkans' Heritage of Hate." *Time,* 12 April 1999.

Nordland, Rod. "In Milosevic's Wake." *Newsweek,* 9 April 2001.

Nordland, Rod, and Zoran Cirjakovic. "Cold-blooded Justice." *Newsweek,* 24 January 2000.

Perlez, Jane. "Milosevic Should Face Trial by Hague Tribunal, Bush Says." *The New York Times,* 2 April 2001.

"As Expected, Belgrade Wins 'Cooperative' Seal From U.S." *The New York Times,* 3 April 2001.

"Powell, on First Balkans Trip, Warns Against Fresh Violence." *The New York Times,* 14 April 2001.

Ramo, Joshua Cooper. "Bagging the Butcher." *Time,* 9 April 2001.

Ratnesar, Romesh. "Terrain of Terror." *Time,* 12 April 1999.

Ross, Stewart. *The War in Kosovo.* Austin, Tex.: Raintree Steck-Vaughn Publishers, 2000.

"Rough Justice in Belgrade." *Time,* 24 January 2000.

Schmemann, Serge. "How to Face the Past, Then Close the Door." *The New York Times,* 8 April 2001.

Silber, Laura, and Allan Little. *Yugoslavia: Death of a Nation.* New York: TV Books, 1995.

Thompson, Mark. "The Pentagon's Plan." *Time,* 12 April 1999.

"Tito Dies at 87; Last of Wartime Leaders." Reuters, 5 May 1980.

Todorovic, Alex. "From Villa to Prison Cell." *U.S. News & World Report,* 16 April 2001.

Todorovic, Alex, and Kevin Whitelaw. "A Mobster, a Robber, a Serbian Hero." *U.S. News & World Report,* 31 January 2000.

Walters, E. Garrison. *The Other Europe: Eastern Europe to 1945.* New York: Dorset Press, 1988.

Whitelaw, Kevin. "Endgame in Belgrade." *U.S. News & World Report,* 9 April 2001.

"The World's Most Dangerous Man." Transcript of *Frontline* broadcast, produced by Pippa Scott for WGBH-TV, Boston, Mass., 26 May 1998.

Yancey, Diane. *Life in War-Torn Bosnia.* San Diego, Calif.: Lucent Books, 1996.

Arkan Shot Dead. By Vana Susa
  [http://www.ce-review.org/00/2/susa2.html]

Arrest of Slobodan Milosevic
  [http://www.aimpress.org/dyn/trae/archive/data/200104/10405-004-trae-beo.htm]
  [http://www.cnn.com/2001/WORLD/europe/04/01/milosevic.arrest.06/]

The Balkans. ABC News
  [http://abcnews.go.com/sections/world/balkans_content/]

The Balkans. North Park College, Chicago, Illinois
  [http://campus.northpark.edu/history/WebChron/EastEurope/Balkans.html]

Balkans Special Report. The Washington Post
  [http://www.washingtonpost.com/wp-srv/inatl/longterm/balkans/overview/overview.htm]

Bloody Weekend in Drenica. By Dejan Anastasijevic For Independent Yugoslavia
  [http://www.cdsp.neu.edu/info/students/marko/vreme27.html]

History of Serbia
  [http://www.decani.yunet.com/serhist.html]

How the War Started. By Alan F. Fogelquist, Department of History, UCLA
  [http://www.its.caltech.edu/~bosnia/doc/start.html]

Interview with Radovan Karadzic. By Rob Siebelink, Reporter for Drentse
  Courant-Groninger Dagblad
  [http://users.bart.nl/~papafinn/kara-gb.html]

Kosovo Atrocities Coordinated from the Top, Says Human Rights Group.
  The Guardian
  [http://www.guardian.co.uk/yugo/article/0,2763,581789,00.html]

Montenegrins Split on Independence. By James Kliphuis, Radio Netherlands
  [http://www.rnw.nl/hotspots/html/montenegro010423.html]

Montenegro After the Elections. AIM Press
  [http://www.aimpress.org/dyn/trae/archive/data/200104/10426-007-trae-pod.htm]

Newsmaker: Richard Holbrooke. PBS NewsHour
  [http://www.pbs.org/newshour/bb/europe/july-dec98/holbrooke_7-7.html]

Poetry of Radovan Karadzic. Frontline
  [http://www.pbs.org/wgbh/pages/frontline/shows/karadzic/radovan/poems.html]

Serb Policeman Denies Killing Arkan. CNN
  [http://www.cnn.com/2000/WORLD/europe/10/17/belgrade.arkan/]

Serbs Jailed for Arkan Killing. CNN
  [http://europe.cnn.com/2001/WORLD/europe/10/26/yugoslavia.arkan/]

Slobo! We Will Never Give You Up! By Catherine Lovatt, Central Europe Review
  [http://www.ce-review.org/01/13/lovatt13.html]

South Slavic Languages. Encyclopedia of Linguistics
  [http://www.fitzroydearborn.com/chicago/linguistics/sample-language.php3]

Statement of President Slobodan Milosevic on the Illegitimacy of The Hague Tribunal
  [http://www.icdsm.org/more/aug30.htm]

Surging Insurgency: The Kosovo Liberation Army. PBS NewsHour
  [http://www.pbs.org/newshour/bb/europe/july-dec98/kla_7-15.html]

Ten Charged in Belgrade over Arkan Murder. CNN
  [http://www.cnn.com/2000/WORLD/europe/07/18/yugo.arkan.charges.reut/]

Two Kings Battle. Frontline
  [http://www.pbs.org/wgbh/pages/frontline/shows/karadzic/bosnia/twokings.html]

War Crimes in Yugoslavia. U.S. Department of State
  [http://www.dssrewards.net/english/warcrimes/karadzic.html]

Who Killed Arkan? By Laura Rozen, Salon Magazine
  [http://www.salon.com/news/feature/2000/01/17/arkan/]

Zeljko Raznatovic. Articles by Joe Havely, Paul Wood and Jim Fish, BBC
  [http://news.bbc.co.uk]

HAL MARCOVITZ is a journalist for *The Morning Call,* a newspaper based in Allentown, Pennsylvania. He has written more than 30 books for young readers, including biographies of Robin Williams, Ron Howard, and Al Sharpton for Chelsea House Publishers. He lives in Chalfont, Pennsylvania, with his wife, Gail, and daughters, Ashley and Michelle.